# *Maternal Connections*

## When Daughter Becomes Mother

Edited by Joan Garvan and Kandee Kosior

DEMETER

**Maternal Connections**
When Daughter Becomes Mother
Edited by Joan Garvan and Kandee Kosior

Copyright © 2022 Demeter Press

Individual copyright to their work is retained by the authors. All rights reserved. No part of this book may be reproduced or transmitted in any form by any means without permission in writing from the publisher.

Demeter Press
PO Box 197
Coe Hill, Ontario
Canada
K0L 1P0
Tel: 289-383-0134
Email: info@demeterpress.org
Website: www.demeterpress.org

Demeter Press logo based on the sculpture "Demeter" by Maria-Luise Bodirsky www.keramik-atelier.bodirsky.de

Printed and Bound in Canada

Cover artwork: *An Offering* by Jasmine Symons
Cover design and typesetting: Michelle Pirovich
Proof reading: Jena Woodhouse

Library and Archives Canada Cataloguing in Publication
Title: Maternal connections : when daughter becomes mother / edited by Joan Garvan and Kandee Kosior.
Names: Garvan, Joan, editor. | Kosior, Kandee, 1967- editor.
Description: Includes bibliographical references.
Identifiers: Canadiana 20220260486 | ISBN 9781772584080 (softcover)
Subjects: LCSH: Mothers and daughters. | LCSH: Mothers and daughters—Anecdotes. | LCSH: Motherhood. | LCSH: Motherhood—Anecdotes. | LCSH: Mothers. | LCSH: Mothers—Anecdotes.
Classification: LCC HQ755.86 .M38 2022 | DDC 306.874/3—dc23

With love and gratitude to our mothers
and those who have cared for us over generations,
time and place.

May the significance of the work of care be
further understood and truly valued through our social
and cultural frameworks.

# Acknowledgments

This book would not exist without our team of generous, enthusiastic, and like-minded supporters. We wish to warmly thank Andrea O'Reilly, founder and senior editor of Demeter Press, for providing us the opportunity to put together this edited collection. We are especially grateful to our copy editor, Jesse O'Reilly-Conlin, and to our reviewers, who provided helpful feedback.

We were thrilled with the enthusiastic response we received to the call for papers and heartily thank the authors for sharing their personal narratives, artistic creations, professional observations, and academic inquiries. We want to thank Leanne Sheeran, Linda K. Jones, and Anthony Welch for their review of the related literature, and we are indebted to Nancy Chodorow, Wendy Hollway, Alison Stone, and Petra Bueskens, among others, for their continuing work in this regard.

We sincerely thank our colleagues and friends who listened, advised, and encouraged us as we went through the book-editing process: Leslie Hood, Annette Styles, Eva Byron, Lin Baron, Sydney Bell, Saverina Allevato, Leeann Debert, Jana Bulhman, and Christine Zyla with a special thanks to Denise Burton for her suggestion for the title *Maternal Connections*.

We express our heartfelt gratitude to our families, who inspire and support us in this journey of discovery: Barry York, Hannah Garvan, Joseph York, Sarra Swarmi, Lesley Berry, Donalda Kosior, Jim Powers, Emily Powers, Clayton Powers, and Benen Powers.

# Artist's Note

Jasmine Symons

## *An Offering*

A work belonging to the PhD research project titled *Ambiguity Makes Sense,* which explores the creative relationship between mothering and painting.

I wonder how far back a mother's sensory memory can be traced and how far into the future that sensory memory becomes interlaced. Since becoming a mum, I feel both porous and in excess of my own lived time. Lace doilies and a hand painted plate are the oldest (non-human but alive) remnants of my matriarchal heritage.

# Contents

**Introduction**
*Joan Garvan*
13

**Part I.**
**Sociology**
29

**1.**
"Your Daughter Should Know What an Iron Is by Now":
A Feminist Examination of the Role of a Mother's Mother
in the Development of the Maternal Self.
*Lauren Hansen*
31

**Part II.**
**Life Story**
41

**2.**
"A Black Daughter Like Me": Breaking the Curse
of Matrilineal Fragmentation"
*Mali Collins*
43

**3.**
"I Do Not Want to Become You": A Walk through the
Relationship between Mother and Daughter Intersected by
Motherhood and Feminism
*Sabela Losada Cortizas*
51

**4.**
Woman-as-Child-to-the-Mother
*Joan Garvan*
61

**5.**
Mother of Mother of Mother
*Andi Spark*
67

**6.**
Becoming a Mother Philosopher
*Cassie Premo Steele*
83

**7.**
"Get Something in Your Head, and They Can't Take it Away": Education as a Family Value Passed through Black Mississippi Mothers
*Marcia Allen Owens*
91

**8.**
Liminalities of the Mother
*Jameka Hartley*
103

**9.**
Nitaawigiwin: A Ceremony of Thinking about My Anishinaabeg Mother
*Renee E. Mazinegiizhigoo-kwe Bedard*
115

**Part III.
Ritual, Art, and Literature**
129

## 10.
### Perspectives on Motherhood through the Lens of Postmemory and Artistic Practice
*Sylvia Griffin*
131

## 11.
### Her Face Is My Face, Too: Matrilineal Connection through Art Practice
*Allegra Holmes*
143

## 12.
### Minding the Mother: Intrapsychic Effects of the Mother-Daughter Relationship in Elena Ferrante's *The Lost Daughter*
*Inês Faro*
155

## 13.
### Hija eres y madre serás: Daughters and Their Mothers in Latinx Memoirs by Cherríe Moraga and Anika Fajardo
*Astrid Lorena Ochoa Campo*
165

## 14.
### Maternal Haunting in Elisa Albert's *After Birth*
*Rachel Williamson*
175

**Notes on Contributors**
189

# Introduction

Joan Garvan

> Only by placing each and every woman within the context of her relationships towards the continuum of women she is part of can we truly give voice to long silenced mothers and daughters.
>
> Elzbieta Korolczuk 222

This interdisciplinary collection of chapters has been inspired by Andrea O'Reilly's work on matricentric feminism, a form of feminism that begins with the mother and takes seriously the work of mothering. The first chapter is a sociological overview drawing from interviews with five women on their relationship with their mother to explore influences and outcomes for their sense of self after they too became mothers. Three of the chapters are literary critiques, with some drawing from an emergent body of work from within sociology and psychoanalysis on maternal subjectivity. The strength of the collection is in the autobiographical nature of most of the chapters. There is clearly a significant and abiding connection between mothers and their daughters, which is pertinent to the experience of women after the birth of a child. In the early twenty-first century, when many new mothers grapple with a sense of self, it is important to recognize and reflect on the foundational nature of these maternal connections.

We have second-wave feminists to thank for unearthing a myriad of materials on women—including within the areas of history, philosophy, politics, health, and science, with increasing attention being given to the connection between women and their mothers after they too become a mother (Chodorow; Stone; Pascoe; Hirsh; Green). Over time, much of the documentation on maternal connections has been written by men, with some brief but notable exceptions (Phillips). Scholars such as Tillie Olson, Adrienne Rich, Toni Morrison, and Nancy Chodorow prompted a concern with the experience of women as mothers. This academic output was followed by the creation of Demeter Press, which provides a significant avenue for the circulation and publication of an international body of research and writing on the experience of women as mothers. However, as O'Reilly points out, there is a continuing reluctance within wider feminist circles to recognize and respond to the call.

The connections between mothers and their daughters have a social and cultural context; these relationships have been couched within a milieu that sanctioned male authority over women as well as a divide, through law and everyday practice, between the public, social, and political world and the private realm of marriage and the male-headed family. Mothers were expected to pass on to their daughters a maternal role that necessarily included the care and protection of their infants and children, along with the management of homes and families. Mothers often modelled the maternal role, even if they too might have been ambivalent or sceptical about the constraints; anything else was read as a failure to care.

Mid-twentieth-century second-wave feminism led to a daughter-centric perspective taken by writers, such as Nancy Friday in *My Mother Myself*, which questioned these mother-daughter associations. Furthermore, through a combination of sociology and psychoanalysis, Nancy Chodorow provided a framework for understanding psychological processes that perpetuate the reproduction of mothering. Her work led into further avenues by way of understanding maternal subjectivity, the complex and foundational mother-infant connections, and the value of recognizing and responding to the mother-daughter relationship. A parallel interest in the mother-infant connection within psychoanalysis, led by John Bowlby's work on bonding, focused on outcomes for infants and children rather than the mother (Hollway, "Family Figures"; Pascoe). This led into the influential study, *Ghosts in the Nursery,* that recognized the influence of mothers' experience of infancy and childhood, but, again, it was primarily concerned with outcomes for infants and children—an emphasis that remains today in policy and practice. Nevertheless, an emergent field on maternal subjectivity features the significance of the mother's connection with her own mother after the birth in terms of the woman's sense of self (Stone; Hollway; Benjamin).

Chodorow's continuing work as a psychotherapist, Daniel Stern's notion of the mother-infant constellation, Jessica Benjamin's work on intersubjectivity, and Alison Stone's understandings of maternal subjectivity all highlight the need to understand interactions and outcomes for both mother and baby. Yet a recent literature review by Leanne Sheeran, Linda Jones and Anthony Welch brought to light a continuing gap in the related research and thus the need for a collection such as this. The themes taken up in this multidisciplinary approach to maternal connections are discussed below. I hope this work will prompt reflection and further consideration being given to connections and disconnections between generations of mothers and the effect of birth and mothering on both the mother and child.

## A Brief History of the Social and Cultural Context of Maternal Connections

The unfolding historical record is relevant here. In her landmark BBC series *The Ascent of Woman*, the historian Amanda Foreman takes the subjugation of women back to the Enmetena and Urukagina Cones (2400 BC), in which the right was written into law to smash a woman's teeth if she spoke too loudly. In Ancient Greece and Rome, women were beholden to their fathers and their husbands; however, either through good luck, good fortune, or good management, some women took advantage of their position and, for a time, guided the course of their own history (Phillips 241-42).

A significant Greek myth in this regard is that of Demeter. The goddess of the harvest sought revenge for Hades stealing her daughter by causing plants to wither and die over the part of the year that Persephone was called to spend in the underworld. The Electra complex is equally drawn from a Greek myth that tells of the brother Orestes and sister Electra plotting the death of their mother as revenge for their father's murder (Phillips 230-2).

The ascendency of Christian belief throughout Europe brought the doctrine of the virgin birth and the theological divide between the mind and the body (Lloyd), which included a belief in a pure, heavenly celestial realm that was separate from all things temporal. Godliness was associated with purity, and female sexuality needed to be regulated and constrained, so as not to tempt men away from an eternal hereafter. Christine de Pizano (1364-c1430), France's first woman of letters, was widowed with small children. She earned a living through her writing and proposed that although mothers may want their daughters to read and write, their primary responsibility "was to ensure their daughters' moral behaviour, that is, to preserve their chastity" (Deakins 67).

Throughout much of European history daughters have been beholden to their mothers. Marriage was practiced in both Ancient Greece and Rome, and up into the nineteenth century, marriage was primarily about solidifying family alliances, status, and wealth (Coontz). Women, who had few to no individual rights, were pawns to be traded or subsumed to wider sociopolitical concerns. Women who were in positions of influence were confronted with the need to coerce or manipulate their daughters' marriage options to maintain their own privilege. Mothers were most often the enforcers of patriarchal practice with little option for deviation (Coontz 53-60). Alliances between kingdoms were sealed through marriage. The union between Cleopatra and Anthony, for example, was more about political alliance than love (Coontz 62). The kings and queens of England and Europe became intimately connected through allegiance in marriage and the children who followed.

The mother's role was to teach her daughters to be good wives, to pass on the required skills, to attend to the domestic realm, to manage cooks and servants for wealthy families, as well as to cook, clean, sew, and care for infants and children. Further to this was the need for women to be chaste and obedient and to be moral and virtuous, which are attributes commonly associated with the good mother. If daughters went into the monastery, there was the possibility for learning—for example, Hildegard of Bingen who was a writer, composer, philosopher, and Christian mystic of the Middle Ages.

Up into the twentieth century and in some places the early twenty-first century, if parents were not married at the time of birth, the status of the child was recorded as illegitimate, which carried a stigma for both mother and child and left women unprotected in law. Women who conceived outside of marriage were shunned and considered ineligible wives. Thus, infanticide was commonly practiced over millennia. Churches and the religious contested the practice with the establishment of baby farms and orphanages to provide an alternative (Thurer).

During the 1970s, much of the related literature critiquing the family was daughter focused. Classics, including Germaine Greer's *Female Eunuch*, talked about abolishing marriage and were concerned with a woman's experience of her body. *Damned Whores and God's Police* by Ann Summers focused on the divide between women, which was a continuation of earlier methods that effectively herded women into marriage and perpetuated the notion that women were moral guardians. Nancy Friday was concerned with breaking away from the repressive sexual norms that had been reinforced through the life of her mother. She chose not to have children partly, she said, because she did not want to pass on to them the anxious, nervous, and frightened person she had seen in her mother (459).

Chodorow's analysis was part of a swathe of texts that set out to describe the experience of daughters. The landmark work by Rich, *Of Woman Born*, through a mix of history, poetry, and creative writing, located and described her experience of being a mother. In her work, Rich speaks about her relationship with her own mother: "For years, I felt my mother had chosen my father over me, had sacrificed me to his needs and theories" (222). When Rich's first child was born, she was barely in touch with either her mother or her father: "I could not admit even to myself that I wanted my mother, let alone tell her how much I wanted her" (222). Rich came to understand the guilt that came between herself and her mother—something that accompanies an institutionalization of motherhood whereby unrealized expectations and aspirations for the child were most often placed at the feet of the mother. She felt she had not done her job well enough. But further to this, Rich saw that her mother's guilt for not producing a son for her husband was exacerbated when confronted with her rebellious daughter with her son beside her. Later in life, the relationship between Rich and her mother was renewed, and they were able to talk through their trials. She describes these as "infinitely healing conversations with her in which we could show all our wounds, transcend the pain we had shared" (224).

The second-wave daughter-centric trend of the literature, nevertheless, gave way to a mother-centric focus. Most have been concerned to describe or analyse the experience of being a mother, with surprisingly little reference to connections with their own mother in such titles as *The Mother Trip, Dispatches from a Not So Perfect Life, Secret Mothers' Business, The Motherload,* and many more. It is interesting to note that the more recent collection *What My Mother and I Don't Talk About,* is predominantly daughter-centric, with the exception of Carmen Maria Machado, who speaks about a reluctance to have children, in light of her life experience with her mother. Furthermore, the novel *Burnt Sugar,* a short-listed title for the 2020 Booker Prize, includes reflections on the mother-daughter relationship after the birth of a child.

## Mother-Infant Connections, Feminism, Psychoanalysis, and Maternal Subjectivity

Although the 1975 study *Ghosts in the Nursery* recognizes and responds to harmful mothering practices, the emphasis is on disrupting patterns of behaviour for the health and wellbeing of infants and children. The authors speak of a difference between parents who had lived through tormented childhoods, those who had recognized and acknowledged their pain and took measures so as not to pass on the experience, and others who had repressed the experience and were thus bound to repeat the past with their own children (420). Selma Fraiberg et al. argue that through reflection and understanding, we can not only disrupt the harmful practices passed on from mother to child but also enhance the foundational mother-child relationship.

A medicalization of birth throughout the twentieth and early twenty-first century has contributed to diminishing attention being given to the social, cultural, and psychological factors that are necessarily played out in mother-infant interactions (Fox et al.). There is a continuing emphasis on infants and children with the effect of making mothers invisible, particularly during the postnatal phase. While women are trying to do it all, there are serious concerns related to the transition to parenthood, which include high levels of depression and anxiety as well as commonly referenced issues related to identity (Garvan). These concerns are most often spoken about as "matrescence"

—the physical, emotional, hormonal, and social transition to becoming a mother, or more recently referenced as "reproductive identity" (Athan). This neglect of the needs of mothers is highlighted in the earlier referenced study by Sheeran et al., who find that there was a "paucity of research" on a mother's experience of infancy and her connection with her own mother (31).

Rich makes the critical distinction between motherhood, a patriarchal construct, and mothering, the everyday work of care. Feminist critiques of psychoanalysis have fostered a renewed focus on maternal subjectivity, including Benjamin's use of the notion of intersubjectivity to describe mother-infant interactions. Rozeka Parker's work on maternal ambivalence recognizes the significance of the mother's experience of infancy, as does Hollway's understanding of the development of a capacity to care. Lisa Baraitser's philosophical reflections on an ethics of interruption recognises the complex mother-infant dynamics that necessarily draw on the mother's experience of infancy; encounters with her own mother that Raphal-Leff describes as healing early scars (54). Both Baraitser and Stone engage with Julia Kristeva's notion of "matricide"—or the death of the mother that is said to have taken place through western philosophical traditions whereby the subject of the woman as mother goes unrepresented. Stone posits that maternal subjectivity is tied to the mother's experience of being mothered:

> To mother and to relate to her child from a maternal position, the mother must reinhabit the realm of bodily intimacy and dependency. Moreover, to do so the mother has to draw upon and reactivate her own, hitherto largely forgotten, history of maternal body relations. The mother re-enters her own maternal past, which comes alive for her again in the new form of her present-day relationship with her child. (1)

Kristeva and Stone continue to work at repair. Stone emphasizes the importance of recognizing and responding to the reworking of a mother's experience of infancy, after becoming a mother herself:

> I suggest that for maternal subjectivity to be possible the *mother* must be able to assume a subject position distinct from that of the daughter. Mothering is a variation on being a daughter, in so far as the mother replays with her child her own maternal past. Yet

this replaying of the past is a replaying *with a difference.* This difference makes the maternal position a distinct one, and brings with it various further implications for the distinctive structure of maternal subjectivity. (5)

Chodorow maintains that her clinical practice confirms her theoretical understandings on the reproduction of mothering. The mother necessarily becomes a prime influence in her daughter's renewed sense of self when she too becomes a mother and is captured in the phrase "the personal is personal" ("Women Mother Daughters" 50). Chodorow discusses this dynamic: "Mothering and maternal identity are internal mother-daughter experiences, and this maternal sense of self, being a mother, having been mothered—goes through the life cycle" ("Women Mother Daughters" 54). The realization of these influences is necessarily played out differently, depending on the relationship and the particularities of each case—a dynamic referenced by Chodorow as "maternality." Whether or not each woman has children or not, she "brings something of daughter-mother/mother-daughter to her concerns, conflicts, and sense of self" ("Women Mother Daughters" 63).

Stern's conception of the "motherhood constellation," which has become a primary source within midwifery and maternal and child health, recognizes the mother's relationship with her own mother as a major influence in the mother's renewed sense of self, yet this remains to be integrated into everyday practice within the health-related fields. These dynamics are documented in Carla Pascoe's series of interviews with Australian women on their relationship with their mother after they had become mothers. She highlights differences in the experience across time, focusing on the social and cultural context, with interviewees who had become mothers from the 1950s and 1960s, across the decades, and up to 2015. Pascoe took a matricentric approach to her study, referencing matrilineal influences, and she couched these life course stories in terms of maternographies—that is "a woman's life story where her maternal memories are explicitly privileged and highlighted, within a matricentric feminist frame" (14). Amber Kinser cites the notion of matrophobia, which is the fear of becoming one's mother, a process that can be identified while reading these chapters. Studies such as these provide a context for many of the in-depth, descriptive, and mostly autobiographical reflections on the mother-to-mother connection that has sadly been given far too little serious attention generally by the related services.

Two of the contributors to this volume reflect on the loss of their mother either before the birth of their first child or in the early years afterwards. This loss was profound. They felt cheated of the opportunity to share with their mother the experience of the mother-child bond along with their new sense of self. Hope Edelman explores these dynamics in her publication *Motherless Mothers*. Edelman lost her mother at the age of seventeen and had previously written on being a motherless daughter, reflections that she reappraised after she herself had become a mother. She longed for the practical and emotional support often provided by mothers, especially in the early years after the birth. She found that becoming a mother had reunited them in a way she never expected (xxxii). Edelman reviews the scanty related literature and draws together themes from the multiple interviews she carried out with women who were motherless mothers.

## Outline of Chapters

The stories in this collection span literary, autobiographical, sociological, and psychological dimensions in their exploration of the connections between women who become mothers and their mothers. The collection represents a turning back, a reappraisal of the relationship between daughters who have become mothers and their mother. The authors have a renewed appreciation and understanding of their mother and how this intersects with their own sense of self. In her chapter, Lauren Hansen takes a sociological approach and highlights findings from a series of interviews with women reflecting on the attributes and practices they will carry forward or discard from their experience of being mothered. The graphic chapter by Andi Spark depicts continuity and change across three generations, and chapters by Cassie Premo Steele, Sabela Losada Cortizas, Mali Collins, Marcia Allen Owens, Jameka Hartley, and me use creative writing to describe the life-course experience. Renee E. Mazinegiizhigoo-kwe Bedard outlines Anishinaabeg ceremonial practices that honour and represent maternal connections, and Sylvia Griffin and Allegra Holmes demonstrate how art and craft can both assist in working through and carrying forwards maternal stories. In contrast Inês Faro, Astrid

Ochoa-Campo, and Rachel Williamson use a combination of literary critique, feminist theory, and post-Freudian psychoanalysis to interpret varied texts.

Hansen sees the recognition of the dynamics between daughters and their mothers after the birth of their child as an evolution in understanding of maternal subjectivity. She highlights findings from interviews with women in Melbourne, Australia, and incorporates the notion of maternography and matroreform to describe the delineations her interviewees make between their life choices and influences from their mother. She reflects on similar dynamics within her own life, her thoughts about being mothered, along with an aspiration to influence the lives and practices of her offspring.

Spark graphically contrasts differences and similarities between her mother and her daughter. She reflects on qualities and characteristics of her mother that became important markers in the later days of her mother's life—things that only someone close could know and accommodate. The chapter wonderfully demonstrates the evocative power of the image in telling a story.

The autobiographical chapters are drawn from six different life experiences. Collins, Owens, and Hartley describe their relationship with their mother and maternal connections considering their African American heritage. Collins reflects on the ambiguity she experienced being born Black with a white mother, and Owens speaks about the emphasis on education that had been passed on through her mother and grandmother. Hartley's mother died soon after she became a mother for the first time. She writes poetically about her loss and the significant and abstract connection between them, likening this to the middle-shadow ground between life and death.

Losada Cortizas writes about the effect of embedded and gendered associations with care that she witnessed through her mother's life and believed that she could overcome. The experience is captured in the phrase "I don't want to become you," but she realized there was no reprieve, and it was her mother who was there for her by way of support and comfort. Steele emphasizes the differences between mother and daughter while couching her exposition within philosophical understandings. Steele grew up at a distance from her mother who had been chasing a career in philosophy and a social life with colleagues, but she has clearly taken a string from her mother's bow drawing from philosophers to illustrate a point. When she was young, she drew a line in the sand by renaming herself and continued her life at a distance. She was shaken, however, at the thought of coming out to her mother, telling her that she was gay, only to be greeted with uncomplicated acceptance.

My short piece is drawn from a conference video presentation in which I describe an understanding of my connection with my mother that was prompted by the birth of my own first child. I believe that my mother was understandably ambivalent about my birth, and I came to think of the effect as broken hearted. It is not that I felt unloved. It was the consequence of pregnancy and birth, particularly for women in mid-twentieth century Australia, that placed mothers in a bind. I think of this in terms of the patriarchal structuring of motherhood, which effectively constrains and disempowers women as well as disrupts communication between mothers and their children.

Renee E. Mazinegiizhigoo-kwe Bedard explains the significance of the Anishinaabeg ceremonial practice of nitaawigiwin, which involves the collection and burial of the placenta and the amniotic sac. She took part in these practices as a way of respecting and evoking her connection with her late mother, her ancestral grandmothers, and her daughter. Griffin and Holmes draw from their work as artists to reflect on their maternal connections. Griffin's parents were Jews who had survived the Holocaust. They necessarily carried with them dislocation and trauma, events that often became unspeakable and fuelled a kind of postmemory trauma that worked as a barrier between mother and daughter. These were mother-daughter dynamics that Griffin reflected on after she had become a mother in the hope that she might understand and overcome the effect. This ambition, however, was thwarted when her mother was diagnosed with cancer and passed away soon after the birth of Sylvia's child. Griffin used embroidery and knitting as a means of reflection, representation, and repair; she created and recreated items that held meaning and connection. Holmes has been inspired by the domestic decorative arts that were practiced by her maternal forebears. She uses the example of crocheted doilies, bedspreads, and the occasion her maternal great-grandmother walked to a nearby village so as to buy the material for a veil for her daughter's Holy Communion to demonstrate the connection across time and place that is carried through these objects—items that often became family heirlooms. Holmes proposes that creations such as these empower through an assertion of the self and provide for matrilineal connection across generations. She goes on to describe her own creation that references her great grandmother's story with plans to pass this on to her daughter.

Faro, Ochoa-Campo, and Williamson's chapters are literary critiques. Faro explores the notion that Leda, the central character in Elena Ferrante's novel, *The Lost Daughter*, reflects on her subjectivity as a mother. She cleverly draws from psychoanalysis, feminist theory, and literary critique to develop her argument. Leda reflects on her relationship with her own mother and, in turn, her connection with her two daughters. These dynamics are prompted through her projections and reactions towards a mother-daughter-doll trio (mother-daughter-baby) that she encounters on the beach during the summer break.

Williamson's critique is likewise centrally concerned with the subjectivity of Ari, the main character in Elisa Albert's novel *After Birth*, which she depicts as a form of maternal haunting. Ari is overwhelmed by the requirements and expectations of motherhood, particularly in terms of her sense of self. These feelings take her back to her toxic relationship with her own manic and abusive mother and because Janice, her mother, had passed away, Ari rehearses a series of imagined conversations. Drawing from Stone's work, Williamson argues that the author foregrounds the complex dynamics of mothers that necessarily engage with her experience with her own mother. The narrative provides for resolution by way of a connection with a friend who becomes a surrogate maternal figure and assists the process of reparation.

Ochoa-Campo features Cherrie Moraga's *Native Country of the Heart* and Anika Fajardo's *Magical Realism for Non-Believers*, both Latinx memoirs, to explore issues of race, gender, class, and migration as factors that are played out through the mother-daughter relationship after the daughters themselves become mothers. The daughters in each of the novels reflect on their relationship with their own mother considering the difficulties they faced as women in a foreign land and by way of narrating their own story.

I hope the text will prompt reflection and deepen relationships between generations of women who mother and that it will generate research and enhance understandings of maternal connections.

## Works Cited

Athan, Aurelie M. "Reproductive Identity: An Emerging Concept." *American Psychologist*, vol. 75, no. 4., 2020, pp. 445-56.

Baraitser, Lisa. *Maternal Encounters: The Ethics of Interruption*. Routledge, 2009.

Benjamin, J. *Like Subject, Love Object Essays on Recognition and Sexual Difference*. Yale University Press, 1995.

Chodorow, Nancy. *The Reproduction of Mothering: Psychoanalysis and the Sociology of Gender*. University of California Press, 1978.

Chodorow, Nancy. "Women Mother Daughters: The Reproduction of Mothering After Forty Years." *Nancy Chodorow and The Reproduction of Mothering: Forty Years On*, edited by Petra Bueskens. Palgrave Macmillan, 2020, pp. 49-80.

Coontz, Stephanie. *Marriage, a History How love conquered Marriage*. Penguin Books. 2005.

Deakins, A. "Mothers and Daughters: Glimpses through Time." (ed) *Mothers and Daughters Complicated Connections across cultures*, edited by A. Deakins, R. Bryant Lockridge and H. Sterk, University Press of America, 2012, pp. 61-88

Edelman, Hope. *Motherless Mothers: How Mother Loss Shapes the Parent We Become*. Hodder Australia, 2006.

Doshi, Avni. *Burnt Sugar*. Hamish Hamilton, 2020.

Fedler, Joanne. *Secret Mothers' Business: One Night, Eight Women, No Kids, No Holding Back*. Allen and Unwin, 2006.

Filgate, Michele, editor. *What My Mother, and I Don't Talk about Fifteen Writers Break the Silence*. Simon and Schuster, 2019.

Foreman, Amanda. *The Ascent of Woman*. YouTube, December 2020, www.youtube.com/watch?v=W1tVtEMKGAY. Accessed 27 June 2022.

Fox, Haylee, et al. "Evidence of overuse? Patterns of obstetric interventions during labour and birth among Australian mothers". *BMC Pregnancy and Childbirth*, vol. 19, no. 226, 2019, pp. 1-8

Fox, Faulkner. *Dispatches from a Not-So-Perfect Life or How I Learned to Love the House, the Man, the Child*. Harmony Books, 2003.

Fraiberg, Selma, Edna Adelson, and Vivian Shapiro. "Ghosts in the

Nursery: A Psychoanalytic Approach to the Problems of Impaired Infant-Mother Relationships." *Journal of American Academy of Child Psychiatry*, vol. 14, no. 3, 1975, pp. 387-421.

Friday, Nancy. *My Mother/My Self: The Daughter's Search for Identity*. Fontana/Collins, 1986.

Garvan, J. *Maternal Ambivalence in Contemporary Australia: Navigating Equity and Care*. Dissertation. Australian National University, 2010.

Green, Fiona. "Matroreform: Feminist Mothers and Their Daughters Creating Feminist Motherlines". *Journal of the Association for Research on Mothering, Mothers, and Daughters*, vol. 10, no. 2., 2008, pp. 11-21

Greer, Germaine. *The Female Eunuch*. MacGibbon and Kee, 1970.

Gore, Ariel. *The Mother Trip: The Hip-Mama Guide to Staying Sane in the Chaos of Motherhood*. Seal Press, 2000.

Hirsh, Marianne. *The Mother/Daughter Plot Narrative, Psychoanalysis, Feminism*. Indiana University Press, 1989.

Hollway, Wendy. *The Capacity to Care: Gender and Ethical Subjectivity*. Routledge, 2006.

Hollway, Wendy. "Family Figures in 20th Century British 'Psy' Discourse." *Theory and Psychology*, vol. 16, no. 4, 2006, pp. 443-64.

Kinser, Amber. "Mothering Feminist Daughters in Postfeminist Times." *Journal of the Association for Research on Mothering, Mothers, and Daughters*, vol. 10, no. 2, 2008, pp. 22-37.

Korolczuk, Elzbieta. "Ginealogy: Towards the Revival of Feminine Genealogies in the Works of Contemporary Polish Artists." *Journal of the Association for Research on Mothering, Mothers, and Daughters*, vol. 10, no. 2, 2008, pp. 211-224.

Kristensen, Caryl, and Marilyn Kent. *The Motherload: When Your Life's on Spin Cycle and You Just Can't Get the Lid Up!* Harper Perennial, 1998.

Lloyd, G. *The Man of Reason: "Male" and "Female" in Western Philosophy*. University of Minnesota Press, 1984.

Morrison, Toni. *Beloved*. Knopf, 1987.

Olson, Tillie. *Mother to Daughter, Daughter to Mother*. Virago, 1984.

O'Reilly, Andrea, *Matricentric Feminism. Theory, Activism, and Practice*. Demeter Press, 2016.

Parker, Rozsika. *Torn in Two: The Experience of Maternal Ambivalence.* Virago, 2005.

Pascoe Leahy, Carla. "The Mother Within: Intergenerational influences upon Australian Matrescence since 1945." *Past and Present*, vol. 246, no. 15, 2020, pp. 263-94.

Phillips, Shelley. *Beyond the Myths: Mother-Daughter Relationships in Psychology, History, Literature, and Everyday Life.* Hampden Press, 1991.

Rich, Adrienne. *Of Woman Born: Motherhood as experience and institution.* Virago Books, 1986.

Sheeran, Leanne, Linda Jones, and Anthony Welch. "Women's Relationships with Their Own Mothers in the Early Motherhood Period." *International Journal of Gender and Women's Studies*, vol. 3. no. 1, 2015, pp. 26-32.

Stern, Daniel. *The Birth of a Mother.* Basic Books, 1998.

Stone, Alison. *Feminism, Psychoanalysis, and Maternal Subjectivity.* Routledge, 2012.

Summers, Ann. *Damned Whores and God's Police: The Colonization of Women in Australia.* Allen Lane, 1975.

Thurer, Shari. *The Myths of Motherhood: How Culture Reinvents the Good Mother.* Houghton Mifflin Company, 1994.

# Part I

*Sociology*

Chapter 1

# "Your Daughter Should Know What an Iron Is by Now": A Feminist Examination of the Role of a Mother's Mother in the Development of the Maternal Self

Lauren Hansen

This chapter examines the role of a mother's mother in her development of a maternal identity through privileging the voices of five mothers of young children in Melbourne, Australia. Mother as an identity mirrors both personal and social realities (Haynes). Tina Miller contends that we are never merely selves; we are always gendered selves who reflect the biological differences between men and women. She argues that mothers work to incorporate a new self, self-as-mother, into their existing self. Some theories have recognized the importance of relationships with significant others in developing women's sense of identity (Gilligan; Jordan).

This chapter draws on interview data collected as part of a more extensive study (see Hansen) conducted during my doctoral studies in social work. The feminist-informed study was interdisciplinary and drew on theoretical constructs from psychology, sociology, women's studies, and social work. Feminist research acknowledges the social context of women in a gendered society where their experience has been devalued or dismissed. Alison Jaggar argues that research should "focus not only on the outer world but also on ourselves and our relation to that world, to examine critically our social location, our actions, our values, our perceptions, and our emotions" (92). A critical outcome of feminist research has been the emergence of women's voices sharing their experiences (Cosgrove and McHugh). Social workers are heavily engaged in family work and know that a comprehensive understanding of the role of the mother in the family system is imperative to good practice. It is important for social work professionals to recognize that mothers are not simply women with children but are mothers whose sense of self is altered to include close others, including their own mother.

## The Mother's Voice

All of the mothers featured in this chapter were cisgender, white women in long-term heterosexual relationships; four were married, and one was partnered. All but one participant was still in a relationship with their first child's father, and all were in part-time employment and have postgraduate degrees. The women in this chapter represent an exceptionally homogenous sample and distinct voice and should not be taken as representative of mothers' experience. Pseudonyms have been used to protect their identity.

Katrina is in her early forties and works part-time. She is a mother of two daughters, aged nine and three, and is married to the father of her youngest child. She lives in metropolitan Melbourne, as does her family of origin. Ursula is in her late thirties and works part time. She is the mother of one daughter, aged four, and is cohabitating with her daughter's father. Her family of origin lives in regional Victoria, and she lives in metropolitan Melbourne. Melissa is in her early forties and is the mother of two daughters, aged four and one. She is married to her children's father and works part time. Melissa lives in a different state to her family of origin. Kerry is in her early forties and has an eight-year-old daughter and two sons, aged four and ten. She is married to her children's father and works part time. She lives in a different country to her family of origin. Belinda is in her mid-thirties and is the mother of three daughters, including a set of twins, aged seven and five, respectively. She is married to the father of her children and works part time. She resides in metropolitan Melbourne, as does her family of origin.

## The Making of a Mother

In her seminal psychoanalytical text, *The Reproduction of Mothering*, Nancy Chodorow argues that women learn to be mothers from their mothers and that gender stereotypes are reproduced within the family. One of the ways that gender norms in motherhood are repeated is through the mother-daughter relationship, as mothers influence their daughters' understanding and experience of motherhood (Bartholomaeus and Riggs). For Katrina, her positive relationship with her mother helped her to establish her mother identity easily. She was aware of the influence of her mother's mothering on her own style:

> I felt very confident about being a mother. I thought, okay, I knew what to do because I thought I had a pretty good role model in my own mother. I never felt any kind of anxiety about it. I always thought that I'd just get on and do it and that it would be challenging but not too difficult, and that's generally how I found it. The funny thing is I don't think I ever directly asked my mum for much advice and stuff. I just remember thinking, what would she have done? What was my experience of childhood? How do I replicate that? That was how I went, really.

Bartholomaeus and Riggs found that while the increase in mothers working outside the home has changed something of how we mother, what has remained constant across the generations is the expectation that the role of the mother should be a central identity for women. This is especially so for heterosexual, middle-class women like Katrina:

> This is probably where I differed with my mother. My mum was a stay-at-home mom. When I put my older daughter into childcare quite young, she was horrified at that. I remember just saying to her, "Mum, the best mother is a happy mother. I want to go back to work because it makes me happy. I'm not going to be neglecting her. I think it would be good for her social skills, I think it'd be good for this, that and the other. What made you happy was being at home, and that's fine. It was a perfectly valid

decision for you to make. You probably would've felt unhappy if you had been forced to work. I'll feel unhappy if I'm forced to stay home."

## Maternal Support during the Early Years

The modest research into the role of mothers in women's mothering experience reveals that for many, their mothers were supportive during the transition to motherhood (Bailey; Darvill et al.; Nelson), with mothers being a source of advice, both solicited and unsolicited (Sheeran). Daughters, however, did not always welcome the advice given by their mothers. For the women in this study, the advice, though well-meaning, was often felt as judgmental of the women's more progressive parenting style. Each of the mothers experienced this differently, however:

> ...Mum was ironing, and Milly came and said, "What's that Nana?" Mum went, "Wow, that just defines it, doesn't it?" I said, "Yes it defines the fact that we see our priorities as getting clothes that we don't have to iron because then you get to spend more time having fun." She said, "Your daughter should know what an iron is by now." (Ursula)

Although Ursula welcomed her mother's well-meaning assistance with her daughter, intergenerational differences sometimes got in the way of what was helpful and what was judgmental. For example, as a busy working mother, Ursula deliberately did not buy clothing that needed ironing, and she also eschewed gender norms when raising her daughter. As a result, Ursula found it difficult to ask her mother for help with her daughter when she felt it would mean judgment or undermine her feminist values. For Melissa, judgment from her mother was seen as mild and well-intentioned, but the impact was still felt "I mean my mum is in Adelaide, she comes over occasionally and stuff, but she is not really judging hard, but she would say stuff like, 'I would do this'. But, it is only advice and I know that she has done it before and I can see quite clearly where she is coming from" (Melissa).

However, while Katrina accepted that her mother was likely judging her mothering choices, she was unbothered by the thought.

My mother's completely not meddling. I think she bites her tongue a lot. She sometimes will say things, but she's not really. I don't really see her often enough. She's a fantastic grandmother. My mother, her focus has just been on grandmothering, which is great because then she just allows me to be the mother and she doesn't tell me how to do it. She doesn't tell me what to do, but she probably does in a subtle way through her grandmothering. (Katrina)

One of the generational changes that may impact mothers' willingness to accept their mother's advice is the ease with which women can now access information on the internet and through professionals. Clare Bartholomaeus and Damien Riggs found that although mothers considered themselves critical sources of advice for their daughters, their daughters relied more on official and professional sources. For others, their mother's absence due to distance or death is keenly felt (Bailey; Sheeran). Steph Lawler found that a mother's absence, in itself, will be significant for her daughter. Several women in my study lived away from their mothers; for Kerry and Melissa, this affected their experience of mothering in the early years. As Kerry articulated:

Sometimes my experience of being a mother was completely different to other people's experience of being a mother which just kind of then made it a bit hard. For me, it would be fantastic to have family support because there are lots of families here in my little social circle that have extended family in Melbourne that do a lot of helping out, and I feel a little jealous about that.

Although the literature speaks of the emotional toll of a mother's absence during her daughter's parenting journey, the women in this study felt the absence on an essentially practical or conceptual level. The idea that she was missing out on important mothering support was significant for Kerry, especially her experience of the early years of parenting with her older children. Kerry adapted to parenting away from her mother with her first two children and had established a solid network of friends who could help with practical tasks, such as school pickups. Similarly, Melissa also experienced the absence of her mother and her parents-in-law on a more practical level: "We don't have family here in Melbourne, my mother lives in South Australia, and my husband's parents live in Sydney, so we haven't had any family support whatsoever, which ... obviously had its challenges, like when kids are sick and that type of thing."

## Remothering, Matroreform, and the Creation of Feminist Motherlines

Although all mothers are daughters, what happens when daughters become mothers themselves? How do they straddle the two roles of those who meet needs and those who have needs (Lawler)? The act of mothering gives mothers pause to reflect on their upbringing and the decisions their parents—particularly their mothers—made, which develops a new understanding of their mother (Fischer; Sheeran). Some mothers seek to replicate their upbringing, whereas others reject it (Hansen). Mothering their children can be experienced as a remothering for some mothers, in which the practices of mothering healed old wounds and established them as a different kind of mother to their own (Hansen; Wong-Wylie). Belinda had to redefine her symbolic relationship with her mother based on her understanding of her mother's capacity to parent and what this meant for her as a mother:

> There's a whole lot of ambivalence there about being depended on by others. So, she [her mother] would say something at the spur of the moment just to get you to go away or shut up or something like that. Just not very dependable and quite self-centred. So, I think my idea of good parenthood, or good motherhood, is very much formed in opposition to [that] ... I think she did the best she could with the psychological resources she had. But she lacked self-awareness or the honesty to get help or change the way she parented. Who knows what kind of parent I'd be if I had a different kind of parent.

According to Gina Wong-Wylie, matroreform is a process through which mothers reclaim their maternal power by eschewing previously held familial beliefs about parenting for new, different practices in keeping with their feminist ideals. Matroreform allows mothers to reflect on and bequeath their principles and practices of feminist mothering to their children (Green). Several of the mothers interviewed engaged in matroreform, none more explicitly than Ursula:

Yeah, well I've been keeping a journal for Milly ... and I've put on the front of it, just to say, "You're not to read this until you're either at least in your twenties or thirties or if you choose to have children." ... There's that thing of if you're not a mom, and you read it, it would appear like, "Oh my god, she's knackered; she hated me." I've put it at the front: This is not to be read by anyone but Milly, and if you read it and you're offended by something because it is personal, it's just literally just me going "Blah" in this journal. It's just a relief to me to kind of go. I'm being honest. I've said, you know I've typed in there saying, "I really don't like you tonight because I'm feeling really overwhelmed, and I don't like you. But I love you." So, it's that kind of thing. (Ursula)

Both Belinda and Ursula commented on specific maternal behaviours they engaged with when parenting their children that directly opposed to how they were parented. They were consciously choosing to engage in different, more nurturing parenting practices. As Belinda explained: "Also, if I say or promise something, [I follow] through on it. I didn't really have that as a child. My mother, ... if you could ever take her to a psychiatrist, [she] would probably be diagnosed with narcissistic personality disorder. She came from a neglectful and abusive childhood. That was her family background." Even though Katrina's matroreform involved the replication of those elements of her mother's mothering that she felt worthy, such as encouragement of independence, for Belinda and Ursula, their matroreform involved the revision of those elements that they experienced as harmful (Green), which focused on the emotional nurturance they felt was lacking in their upbringing. Ursula spoke of modelling healthy expression of anger:

> I think also when I can actually be human around her, when I'm having my grumpy moments that I can define for her that I'm not angry at you, [or] I'm not grumpy at you. This is how I'm feeling right now, and it's just unfortunate that I took it out on you, and I'm sorry, because I never got that as a kid. My parents would be grumpy or angry whatever. It could be something totally not related to me, but I took it personally as a kid. So, again, it's like assessing my parenting.

Another critical component of matroreform is a sensitivity to the possible future impacts of parenting practices on a child's development, particularly regarding the use of power (Green). For some mothers, this manifests as a fear of becoming their mother (Lawler). This anxiety was certainly salient for both Belinda and Ursula as their children grew older. As Brenda articulated:

> I think I live with the constant sort of anxiety that I will unconsciously replicate some of the things that I found unhelpful in my relationship with my parents' parenting—That thirty years from now my kids are going to be sitting on a couch talking to somebody else about [how] "Our mom was just a screw up. I just can't stand the woman." I really, really don't want that to happen. My husband came from a very normal, nurturing family. He says to me: "My mum's a good mum, and I see you parenting, and you're a good mum. It's okay. They're not going to grow up to hate you. You're not twisting their minds. It's okay. It's okay."

## Conclusion

The women in this chapter were deeply impacted by their relationships with their mothers, both positively and negatively. For those who had a problematic experience of being mothered, the experience of raising their children allowed them to remother through the process of matroreform as well as with new feminist motherlines established for their children. In keeping with how I have foregrounded the voices of mothers in this chapter, the last word should go to Belinda. She has been able to carve out a maternal identity separate from the influence of her mother, embracing both her love for her children and acceptance of herself:

> I think it has improved my self-esteem a lot. The background to motherhood for me is having ... both an ambivalent mother but also a fairly ambivalent experience of family. So against that backdrop, having children and discovering that I am capable of being a good mother, of being that good enough mother that is able to form healthy, nurturing bonds with my own children is something of a relief. There's nothing like your children's

uncomplicated love for you, I think. To make you feel like you're okay as a person.

My two children, and the early years of mothering, were the initial inspiration for my research. I have long recognized that my transition from the needer to the meeter of needs allowed me to heal past wounds from my childhood—to remother. But in writing this chapter, I have reflected on my adult relationship with my mother and its influence on my maternal identity. My mother is the inspiration for both the mother and the woman I am. She is a mother, an expert in early childhood education, a feminist, and a progressive. As a single mother, my mother is my partner in parenthood—serving as both a confidant and a guide. Like the women in this study, I have chosen to replicate and reject aspects of her mothering style. I have learned, over time, to develop and trust my own distinct maternal identity.

## Works Cited

Bailey, Lucy. "Refracted Selves? A Study of Changes in Self-Identity in the Transition to Motherhood." *Sociology*, vol. 33, no. 2, 1999, pp. 335-52.

Bartholomaeus, Clare, and Damien W. Riggs. "Daughters and Their Mothers: The Reproduction of Pronatalist Discourses across Generations." *Women's Studies International Forum*, vol. 62, 2017, pp. 1-7.

Chodorow, Nancy. *The Reproduction of Mothering : Psychoanalysis and the Sociology of Gender.* University of California Press. 1978.

Cosgrove, Lisa, and Maureen C. McHugh. "Speaking for Ourselves: Feminist Methods and Community Psychology." *American Journal of Community Psychology*, vol. 28, no. 6, 2000, pp. 815-38.

Darvill, Ruth, Heather Skirton, and Paul Farrand. "Psychological Factors That Impact on Women's Experiences of First-Time Motherhood: A Qualitative Study of the Transition." *Midwifery*, vol. 26, no. 3, 2010, pp. 357-66.

Fischer, Lucy Rose. "Transitions in the Mother-Daughter Relationship." *Journal of Marriage and Family*, vol. 43, no. 3, 1981, pp. 613-22.

Gilligan, Carol. *In a Different Voice: Psychological Theory and Women's Development.* Harvard University Press. 1982.

Green, Fiona Joy. "Empowering Mothers and Daughters through Matroreform and Feminist Motherlines." *Journal of the Motherhood Initiative*, vol. 9, no. 1, 2018, pp. 9-20.

Hansen, Lauren. "The Self-as-Mother in the Preschool Years: An Interpretive Phenomenological Analysis." *Children Australia*, vol. 45, no. 1, 2020, pp. 48-53.

Haynes, Kathryn. "Transforming Identities: Accounting Professionals and the Transition to Motherhood." *Critical Perspectives on Accounting*, vol. 19, no. 5, 2008, pp. 620-42.

Jaggar, Alison M. "Love and Knowledge: Emotion in Feminist Epistemology." *Inquiry*, vol. 32, no. 2, 1989, pp. 151-76.

Jordan, Judith V. *Women's Growth in Diversity: More Writings from the Stone Center.* Guilford Press, 1997.

Lawler, Steph. *Mothering the Self: Mothers, Daughters, Subjects.* Transformations: Routledge, 2000.

Miller, Tina. *Making Sense of Motherhood: A Narrative Approach.* Cambridge University Press, 2005.

Nelson, Antonia M. "Transition to Motherhood." *Journal of Obstetric, Gynecologic, and Neonatal Nursing*, vol. 32, no. 4, 2003, pp. 465-77.

Sheeran, Leanne. *Mum's the Word: A Phenomenological Exploration of Early Motherhood.* Dissertation. RMIT University, 2012.

Wong-Wylie, Gina. "Images and Echoes in Matroreform: A Cultural Feminist Perspective." *Journal for the Association of Research on Mothering*, vol. 8, no. 1-2, 2006, pp. 135-42.

# Part II

*Life Story*

Chapter 2

# "A Black Daughter Like Me": Breaking the Curse of Matrilineal Fragmentation

Mali Collins

For Cuba

It is one o'clock in the morning, and I cuddle my daughter while she nurses. She lies on my knees, which move back and forth, back and forth, rubbing against the bed as they swish. These mundane activities mark these night-time moments together, which easily surpass two hours. These are the nights everyone complains about. The times I was warned about, but they are the sweetest. I look forward to our quiet moments together.

In these moments, I study her. She is so different to my son; she prefers me over her father. Her hair, fine and curly, has perfectly rolled curls, like rich, dark chocolate tuiles. A friend of mine calls her the "golden girl." Her eyes are a deep brown like mine and her father's. My son's are blue. Like my mother's. Everyone said my son looked like me until she came along. Now I see myself. I am reminded of reading Toni Morrison's *The Bluest Eye*. I grabbed it from our bookshelf and tucked it into the sleeping bag I shared with my mom and my older sister, although I barely understood it at the time. *There was a girl with brown eyes, but she wanted blue ones.* Like me.

The book made me feel safe amid the tumult of my daily life. We moved into our new house when I was eight, but it could hardly be called a home. Six of us took up the three beds in the one room that made up one main area. As the house was void of electricity and running water, we read in the candlelight, which in the year 2000 was very different to my peers. As they began to get computers and their own phone lines in their rooms, I struggled to understand how to run a generator to make a phone call. My mom tried to enthuse us by likening it to camping or like the Laura Ingalls Wilder books we had on our shelves. Still, I was not like Laura. I was not like my mother or my sisters. I had brown eyes—or "black" as I was teased. I had black-brown eyes, and I was Black. I wanted blue ones like my mom. I wanted blue eyes like my sisters. But I was not like her or them. They were white, and I was Black.

The built-in bookshelves at the landing of our stairs featured any type of book my mother could get her hands on. Most of them were do-it-yourself building-type books; some were rudimentary architecture guides and books about plant identification. There were large, dusty dictionaries, and the tatters of old school projects that survived the ten-mile journey from the old house to the new house in which we now lived. These projects were a miracle in their own right, as everything we owned was stored underneath the four-point platform consisting of wood stakes and a plywood floor. The blue-tarped roof did not keep the elements out and most certainly could not protect what was underneath. Cleaning out beneath the house would make up my chores for the years after we left our four-bedroom government-subsidized house in the nearby town of less than four thousand people. Dragging out moulded and destroyed garbage bags of my clothes and treasured belongings, like the Cinderella bottle of body spray my grandmother had bought me at the Disney store in Madison. My favourite clothes were now gone. A Barbie that I would have given a loving haircut to was also gone. As an adult, not having an intact birth certificate would become an inconvenience. But not having the material to recall better memories, before we moved into the new house, would manifest as resentment. I need to hold on to memories for myself.

As a mother, I now mourn the school projects, the pictures, and toys that I vividly remember making. I now hold on to everything my kids make, both large and small. I have a few things—such as a card or a project I gifted my grandmother—but nothing from my mother. Nevertheless, the memories remain vivid. I easily draw scenes from my life from as young as three or four years old. I can tell you what I and those around me were wearing and sometimes the proper sequence of events. Smells of wood chips and creosote flood my daily life like a rush of water that moves too rapidly for me to swim. My brother is different. I often recall events or moments that he has successfully blocked. I envy him, even though he often suggests that I recall too much or too easily. "You shouldn't think so much about those things," he insists. I feel that I must, however, simply because he chooses not.

Years later, my mother sent a box of my things by way of my brother. A box of "my" things he relayed to me—objects that would best be kept by me. She came across these things in what I am sure was a large pile of hoarded goods. An eighth-grade art project made of wood, which was painted and assembled to look like a portion of my face. A comically shaped eyebrow glued by a hot-gun on yellow skin stares back at me from a bookshelf in the living room. The eye is blue of course. In the box were also a volleyball trophy and a cheerleading pin; these are the things that made their way back, things reminding me of my former self. She did not want them. The woodstove and her smoking made the pages yellow and dried. Most were covered with a thin layer of soot.

The correlation between these lost objects was the same as what stood between me and Morrison's Pecola.[1] It was something that was lost on my eight-year-old self, who tried to look like anyone else but me. In kindergarten, I begged my mother to dye my hair blond and to call me Ashley. I was always tall, but until I was eight, I was much taller than my twin brother, who now towers over me. I was coy, with long arms, legs, fingers, and toes. These were the things remarked upon when people were surprised that I was Black, as if they had to state the obvious to cover up what offended their eyes. "You—you're so tall," they would say. I started drinking coffee when I was in seventh grade, drinking daily several cups of my mother's strong Folger's coffee, because I had read that caffeine stunts your growth. My hair was dry and unkempt but always slicked back into a high puff on the crown of my head. A few freckles eventually peppered my entire face. They began on the nose and sprawled across the bridge and towards my cheeks like the wings of the gold-plated carvings of Isis. An Egyptian Goddess I was not. My chin was beyond pointy, with large downturned lips and unwieldy eyebrows that I would machete with a dull Bic men's razor I found in our shower. My fifth-grade school photo marks this atrocity—the eyebrows began halfway across my eye, a mistake that I corrected with patience according to my *Seventeen Magazine*. I was an anomaly. I had big teeth that I rarely displayed in pictures or in real life. I was my own person, alone and different

As early as my elementary years, I often worried about what my kids would look like and whether they would hate themselves as much as I hated myself. Would they hide inside during the summer so their skin would not darken by the time they returned to school in the fall? I did not want them to worry about a receding hairline in middle school because they had kept their hair back so that no one would spit compact small pieces of paper at them reading "Wash your hair." I was determined to have white kids. If I have kids with someone white, I reasoned, then my kids will be white. Kids take after their dad. I am black like my dad and my kids will be white like theirs.

I was a budding eugenicist. I was determined to scrap the Blackness from my lineage. If my daughters have kids with a white dad, then their kids will really be white. I had a plan. My twin brother was rewarded for the features we shared. He was a novelty and exotic to the girls at school. He was never without a girlfriend. "Where is my real family? The one who looked like me?" I once asked my mother. "What do you mean?" she responded. "Where is my mom and my dad that look like me?" Questions like this were recitations of the questions I was asked in public, when I was out of earshot with my family, usually at the pool. "What's it like to be adopted?" was one that followed me into high school.

As an adult, I asked my mother what it meant for me to talk about the racism I experienced while growing up. I recalled to my husband how once after a basketball game, a large truck was waiting outside for me and my brother. As we walked to our car, the truck gained speed. We were being chased; they came right next to us and yelled, "NIGGERS!" I was too frozen to respond. My brother hung his head, and as we raced to the car and locked the door, the truck squealed off. I will always remember the eyes of the person driving that black pickup truck. My mother paused, and then replied, "It makes me sad that you had to go through all those things. I had no idea."

At times, I think my mother could not have known. Other times, I grew angry because she had a way to medicate herself from what she was going through. As a teen, I had nothing. And as her alcoholism grew, we would go days without seeing each other and would sometimes go a week without speaking. She would invite her friends over, and even when she was around, they would ask me things like, "So what's it like to be half-coloured?" Her friends would cackle, and she would give a disapproving look and her slow, glassed eyes from being high would say, "Shut up, Bill." But for her, she treated all her kids the same, something she proudly proclaimed, and would use as a weapon against me later in life. I once said that I felt race was a factor in our upbringing. She yelled into the phone: "If I was racist, I would have aborted you." I was the manifestation of her white liberalism. I was relieved, however, that she at least implied, something she always denied, that I was Black.

While pregnant with my daughter, I spoke with a friend who was a mystic. I told her how I could untangle what I had been through and did not want to pass it on to my daughter. I told her about my relationship with my mom and her relationship with her mother. I asked her to make a candle for me that would break the fragmentation in my life. The candle was larger than the palm of my hand and was made with dried rosemary and rose petals. She instructed me to burn it once every night to chant for protection of my womb and to reject negative thoughts. At my baby shower, my grandmother, my mother's mom, flew in. I worked hard to have her fly to California if only for forty-eight hours, and I burned the candle when she arrived. As she leaned over the candle, it flickered and popped. The glass shattered, like a firecracker directly into her eyes. She was fine but demanded I get rid of it. She mumbled something about me having candles with kids in the house.

I remember seeing a photo of my mother featuring a small pregnant belly that if I had not known better could have easily been mistaken for the bulge of her Packers sweatshirt. No photos were taken of her, and her new babies after our birth, which she described as "worse of all the births of her kids." The only thing worse than our surgical birth was the eight centimetre epidural needle being injected into her spinal column. The only thing I know of my birth is horror, which is confirmed in the after-birth photo of my grandmother who held us in the waiting room of my small-town hospital. She held my brother and me, one in each arm, with an exhausted, hackneyed open mouth. Neither smile nor joy came to her face but a sense of relief. Her face details what would become the cold reality of my childhood—a relief to be alive and well but unconvinced and woefully ignorant at what lay ahead.

In the wake of the deaths of George Floyd and Philadelphia Castile[2]—both murdered in the metropolitan area of my college city of Minneapolis—I continue to come to terms with the spectacular instances of gratuitous anti-Black violence. But little is discussed of the anti-Black undercurrent that comes to mind when I hear phrases like "Minnesota Nice"—a saying expressing how outwardly kind, even cloyingly sweet, Minnesotans are. But the more they shower you with hollow niceties, the more they fear or dislike you. Little is said of the intimate violence that occurs in white families who adopt Black children, since they are often seen as a saving grace. As the world protests on behalf of George Floyd, Amaud Arbery, Breonna Taylor, and Tony McDade, and by extension me and my kids, I wonder if it's enough to be in agreement with one side or the other. And although we are estranged, I know that my mother knows I am special; she knows that I am more. I am the dusty mirror that reminds her of what she lost in order for me to find my daughter.

The birth of my daughter was clear. It was different from my son's, whom I had on the floor of a hospital room. The midwife handed him to me like a football through my legs. I held him sideways, afraid he would slip through my grasp onto the damp towels beneath. His body was perpendicular to mine as he moved his eyes sideways to look directly into mine. My first thought was that he looked like my mother. He had the same piercing blue eyes. In the final moments before I had my daughter, I braced myself, calling on all the maternal medicine I could, to be in community with all the other birth people having babies at that very moment. As I was instructed to "grab my daughter out of me." I pulled her up onto my stomach. I tiredly looked at this girl with Josephine Baker eyebrows and the blue eyes that awaited. "Those are the kind that stay blue," my midwife said. However, today, they are brown. She looks just like me.

## Endnotes

1. Pecola Breedlove is the protagonist of Toni Morrison's 1970 novel, *The Bluest Eye*. Pecola is an eleven-year-old girl who drives herself mad trying to fit into white beauty standards and is driven through-

out the novel to somehow turn her eyes blue.
2. George Floyd was killed Minneapolis, MN and Philando Castile in St. Anthony, MN, a suburb of Minneapolis.

## Works Cited

Morrison, Toni. *The Bluest Eye*. 1st ed., Knopf, 2000. Print.

Chapter 3

# "I Do Not Want to Become You": A Walk through the Relationship between Mother and Daughter Intersected by Motherhood and Feminism

Sabela Losada Cortizas

How does motherhood bring to the surface the clashes between desires, gender mandates, bonds, expectations, and freedom? Through analyzing my story as the daughter of a 1970s feminist and as a mother myself, this work explores the mother-daughter relationship from a gender perspective, focusing on how gender socialization models that relationship and the mechanisms that feminism develops to try and overcome it.

## Daughter

After having my son, I fell out with my mother. It did not happen right away; in fact, she was my rock in my decision to have a child and even moved to my house, on another continent, to support me during the birth and postpartum periods. She fed me, washed clothes, woke up at night to help, dressed my wounds, and took care of absolutely everything in the house so that I could dedicate myself to my son and to resting. She mothered me. Thanks to my mother, I had the freedom to choose how I wanted to be a mother.

Nonetheless, a few months later, my feelings suddenly changed. I travelled to Spain with my baby to visit her six months after she had left my house. There, I went from infinite gratitude to rejection and rancour. I could not smile at her or even hug her without it feeling forced. My mind vomited painful memories and infinite reproaches that swirled around a single idea: I do not want to become you.

You may think I'm going to describe one of those sadistic mothers that fill books, movies, and the assortment of pop culture products that litter the planet. No. I recall a happy childhood. I grew up in the countryside, where my parents bought land with friends to build the life they dreamed of. It was the late seventies; the long dictatorship in Spain was finally ending, and everything seemed possible. We lived surrounded by a forest in a house that was always full of people; there was no phone or television, and children and adults played and danced. In the summer, we all swam naked. All voices were heard. They used to say we were building a new world—a free and equal one.

But my parents separated when I was eleven years old and never spoke again. They did not tell me why. Over time, seeing their divergent paths, it seemed impossible that they had ever been together. The abruptness of the separation showed me with crystal clarity two different lifestyles, two available options for being: the masculine model, my father's and the feminine model, my mother's. Opposites.

My mother was mostly sad. At least, I perceived her that way. She would likely say she was tired of running around: from work to the supermarket and then to take me to class, to the doctor's, and then home, where she would cook dinner, help me with exams, and welcome my friends. She was also worried about money, always trying to make it last until the end of the month. She had to fight for a fair salary because there were many months when she was not paid for her job as a teacher in a community-based school. People stopped coming to the house; it was no longer full of gatherings and celebrations. Her new boyfriend lived in another country, and she slowly became isolated. I did not see her smile or enjoy herself, but she took care of everything so efficiently that it drove me to clown around trying to make her laugh. I often felt bad if I did something wrong.

After the separation, my father sank. The feeling of abandonment, and having to start over, drowned him in a period of disorientation. I feared he would not snap out of it, but he did recover. We began to really enjoy spending time together: When I was at his house, his time and energy were exclusively mine, without limits, without obligations or anger. He adored me, and I adored him. He only worked in the mornings. As a respected union representative, his job was well paid, enough that he could take time off frequently. When he moved into town, his social life and availability blossomed. He had a variety of romantic relationships, his circle of friends grew, and he looked happy.

My mother became invisible; my father, in contrast, received more and more recognition. We see from birth how our mothers carry the weight of childrearing as well as other domestic responsibilities, whereas men are celebrated for completing even the smallest of tasks. It could be said that childcaring is the most essential of activities. But considering the sacrifices the job demands and the little importance given to the work of care, who would want to do it? Who wants to be an exhausted adult?

You may think that I will say that my mother was one of those selfless mothers who star in movies and books. But no. The truth is she was never like that. Because in my story, in my genealogy, the person who created the path was not me but her. The person who rebelled against this assigned role, with her body and heart, was my mother. As the daughter of a feminist woman, I grew up confident in my self-worth, confident in the importance of my actions and thoughts, with a conviction that I could carry out my projects for emancipation, whatever they may be. It was her desire to model me in this way. I had no pink princesses or Barbies, nor did I wear heels, which would have held me back from running and climbing trees. My mother's way of life—getting married, divorce, and then finding boyfriend—along with the way she raised me, were the antithesis of the image of my grandmother, who often asked my grandfather for money for her needs.

My mother met my father while studying economics. He was a handsome young man, intelligent and a militant, who opened her eyes to a world completely unknown to her—the struggle of the working class against injustice, inequality, and repression. To pursue a romantic relationship with my father, and at the same time be rid of her family, she had to marry, although she rebelled by arriving at the church in a miniskirt. This was during the 1970s. Their lives were enveloped by political struggle and the creation of a new world. Then I was born. Nobody told me the number of times my mother held me in her bed while my father spent the night out or that she found him in their bed with a female companion or that afterwards she had to wash the sheets or that when my mother wished to do the same, my father tried to stop her by making her feel guilty about neglecting my care. What was then called "free love" was a love that reproduced patriarchal mandates and that varied according to gender. The double standards broke the bubble of the new world project of which she had dreamed. She became sad, and nobody told me why.

My mother and I were on our own in the house in the woods—a house that used to be so full of people but was now an empty and silent house that for me as an adolescent began to feel like a prison. We grew further and further apart, locked in a permanent battle. My mother, the person who had helped me make the signs for the first protest that I organized at school, when girls were forbidden from participating in soccer championships. My mother, who had stones thrown at her by neighbours who would come to yell "whores" when we would swim naked. My mother, whose permission I never had to request, who always said "I support you." That person became frustrated and completely alone. I did not want to see her in my reflection. I made her into the target of my hate and insults. It was not difficult. Freud would have understood perfectly (Stone 48). I will not go into how I rejected my mother for having raised me without a phallus to become hysterical and incomplete. No. What I could not forgive—although I would not have known how to express it—was that she would hide key information about what was happening. Her silence and lies did nothing more than reproduce the law of the father (Martínez 61), which protected men and made me more vulnerable and her guilty of making the world I knew fall to pieces. What I really needed was her honesty and alliance (Friday 4)—qualities that, as we know, are missed in our cultural references about mother-child relationships, full of mothers who die during childbirth, mothers who only take care of their adored male children, and competitive, murderous stepmothers.

I chose to follow my father's model; it was much more attractive. I cut ties with my mother. I decided to build a new way of being a woman, seeing men as equals, eye to eye, occupying their space, and being like them, only feminine. And I did it on a slippery slope. Just as my mother had done before me against the reflection of her mother.

It was not easy to gain respect and be treated as an equal. I was called masculine because my way of living was not appropriate to my sex, including my economic independence, my disinterest in monogamy, and my intention to be a single mother. Although I have been slandered as a harpy or a mad woman (Irigaray 10), I preserved my taste for bringing on my own orgasms, my solitary travels around the world with lovers in every port, my salaries that were larger than my boyfriend's, and maintaining a house of my own. A taxi driver in Buenos Aires noted that I was living abroad with my son, without an executive or diplomat husband dragging me along. I was simply that husband for myself.

## Mother

It has been significant to know that along this entire path, the person who has supported and encouraged me has been my mother. My own motherhood was what reunited us—the woman who wanted to follow the paternal model and the woman who sought maternal care. When I asked her for help to carry forth my pregnancy, to give birth at home, and to bring up a child without a partner; it was the sad mother from my childhood who became the support and embraced my adulthood. It was insubordinate motherhood (Alcalá García 68), which I chose outside of all social conventions, without institutional vehicles, without male intervention. I was taking back motherhood as a feminine experience. As Adrienne Rich articulates:

Without a male adult in the house, without any reason for schedules, naps, regular meal-times, or early bedtimes so the two parents could talk, we fell into what I felt to be a delicious and sinful rhythm.... I remember thinking: This is what living with children could be.... We were conspirators, outlaws from the institution of motherhood; I felt enormously in charge of my life (195).

But a few months later, things changed. Maybe I should have expected it. I had decided to be a mother at a very young age, an age that for the rigid Spanish middle class was better spent on vital objectives such as finishing university, finding a mate, getting a stable job, buying a house, and having fun. I did not want a partner or a house of my own, but I did want to have a child. I knew this decision would have a price, but I never imagined it so high. I lost my job as well as other opportunities for employment, despite my precocious and lengthy career. Life as an independent consultant became difficult, due to lack of availability. I became estranged from activities with friends (our schedules were incompatible), estranged from protests and social centres that were not mother and child friendly, and estranged from entertainment and cultural venues due to their lack of space for children. I could not access my regular haunts (with a baby in arms, a fold-up pram, and baby bag and umbrella) or buy products created for families and couples (like travel packages or supermarket deals), or access many feminist spaces for which the image of a woman with a baby attached to her breast was counterrevolutionary. I became invisible. The mirror threw in my face the reflection of a teary, frustrated, and tired woman. Who was I really if not that sad mother from my childhood? I had transformed into her. So, I escaped her encounter as one would the horror of a bad omen (Sau 28). I do not want to turn into you. I do not want to see myself excluded, stripped of all my projects and vital goals. I do not want to be unhappy and exhausted from lack of time and sleep as well as from the overwhelming responsibility of raising a small boy that I loved more than anyone or thing in the world. Everything seemed impossible. How had I ended up locked up, with my feminism, in the new feminine mystique? Being an insubordinate mother had not saved me from female destiny.

Motherhood is an ambivalent and overwhelming experience: It elevates you, sinks you, destroys and rebuilds: it empties, then fills you with mistreatment and loneliness. In our Western societies, mothers, single or couples, find ourselves suddenly alone and enclosed by four walls, twenty-four hours a day with a baby. Mothers have no one to be with and have no places we can call our own. Matricide—that is, the symbolic negation of the creative authority of mothers (Irigaray 11), the rupture of bonds between women, and the unpaid and unrecognized women's carework (Federici 8) have played a central function in the constitution and reproduction of our capitalist patriarchal system. Our societies are built on the expropriation of female bodies as well as their work, achievements, and children.

## Mothers and Daughters

Gender socialization of girls, including the daughters of feminists, involves negating their mothers, which turns daughters against mothers when as adults they face their mother's reflection in their own motherhood. We daughters hate our mothers when we find ourselves reproducing the patriarchy that we saw in them. Even though I had chosen my father's model, I was a woman like my mother, and my path involved great sacrifice, not because I had chosen it but because it seemed to be on me. Are we, feminist women, trapped in a permanent internal struggle when we want to be mothers?

"So rather than be abandoned you choose to be a mother on your own?" was the question Raquel Schallman, my midwife, asked the day we met. She built a space in her living room, where we pregnant women could express ourselves with our voices and bodies. It was a place where through our senses, we could construct ties and networks with women who were strangers but who nonetheless cared for one another. Such sisterhood between women has been practiced since the 1970s in women's circles throughout the world, but I had never experienced one, despite my feminist militancy beginning in my adolescence. We developed wonderful relationships of support between adults. I currently maintain contact with all my companions, and my son still considers their children "belly siblings" even though more than a decade has gone by, and we live in different countries. Most of my companions separated from their partners when their babies turned two years old; some lived through terrible situations during their pregnancies, and some found themselves raising their children alone, as my mother had warned. Single mothers make networks. We open paths because other women discover in our reflection that there are options for single mothers.

In this context of feminine exaltation, my mother and I were reunited again. Sharing the daily experience of care, slowly, through honesty and vulnerability, my mother and I create space for resistance, support, and renewed alliances. We invent our strategies, just as women have in other times and places (Debold, Wilson, and Malavé). Facing the mandate of mother-daughter separation, we develop a path of reconciliation and share our life stories and survival strategies in this androcentric world. We seek out positive representations of bonds between women and lose the fear of not being the perfect mother or daughter. We show how we have become valued but also confront our doubts and fears in a climate of trust, honesty, and security. Many times, I have felt ashamed of my close bond with my mother, for sharing so many experiences with her, so much intimacy. And despite enjoying her company, her affection and listening, on occasion I have been suspicious of that tenderness, as if it were a sick and neurotic tie. I thought myself a failure, telling myself that those things were just not shared with a mother, but with a man, as if it were something prohibited, even degenerate. An alliance cannot be with anyone but a husband, not even your children. A mother simply cannot be trusted that way; joys are not shared. When it comes to mothers, daughters just complain.

A few weeks before his death, I asked my father for the first time why he and mother had separated. We had never spoken of that difficult subject, but I needed to hear from him. Fathers, as we know, do not talk much, as they feel it is almost obscene to open their feelings to others. He said that people change and these things happen, but he felt that ever since they were young my mother had a sense of competition towards him, something he did not know how to deal with.

Competition. That word resonated in my mind for a long time. Is it not in fact a word that to a large degree defines my relationship with men? I thought that the bond between my parents was theirs only and had nothing to do with me, but it actually determined how I acted towards others throughout the years. Many times I have felt myself competing with men for better grades, higher earnings, more stability, more sexual experiences. If I really think about it, none of my partners could assimilate my achievements with normalcy. Competition appeared as a reproach towards me for having attained achievements that I should not have; it implicated a punishment, penalizing me for having provoked my male partner into feeling disparaged or humiliated.

I am part of that generation of women who encouraged by their mothers, began to fill classrooms in universities, to get better grades than their male counterparts, to have stellar jobs, and to sustain their family through successive crises. We are successful women but are exhausted all the time. Something failed in our liberation. It was not the way they told us it would be. What was missing? Now I have become a feminist mother of boys, but unlike what all the guides and workshops on new masculinities say, I believe that in order to not fall into silly competitions or develop violent complexes, men must learn—even more so than sensitivity and empathy—how to be courageous like women (Rich 215). My mother used to say that men are more cowardly. So I try to raise my children through a variety of references, male and female, outside of the family model and masculine authority. I speak to them with sincerity and believe them always. I name violence and protect them from it while valuing unity, bravery, and care.

## Conclusions

Just as there were no stories about farm women who were not the wives of the farmers, in my childhood books, there were no stories of relationships in which there was protection and support between mothers and daughters. Centuries ago, a woman was slandered as jealous and controlling for wanting to protect her daughter from kidnapping and rape—the story of Demeter. The gender mandate of rivalry and silence for women and the violence of the law of the father are so strong that even in such extreme stories, it is difficult to call things by their name.

We trust that the moment is arriving when as a society, we make care visible and vilify cowardice and damage. We know that through reconciliation and reconstruction, the bond between a mother and daughter can birth a new humanity.

## Works Cited

Federici, Silvia. *Caliban and the Witch: Women, the Body, and Primitive Accumulation*. Autonomedia; Pluto, 2003.

Friday, Nancy. *My Mother/My Self: The Daughter's Search for Identity*. Delacorte Press, 1977.

Debold, Elizabeth, Marie Wilson, and Idelisse Malavé. *Mother Daughter Revolution: From Betrayal to Power*. Addison-Wesley, 1993.

Irigaray, Luce. *Sexes and Genealogies*. Columbia University Press, 1993.

Martínez, Ariel. "La Terceridad Semiótica: Una Crítica Feminista a la Ley Simbólica del Padre en Psicoanálisis". *Revista Aquila*, vol. 9, no 21, 2019, pp. 55-96.

Rich, Adrienne. *Of Woman Born: Motherhood as Experience and Institution*. W. W. Norton and Company, 1995.

Sau, Victoria. *El Vacío de la Maternidad. Madre no hay Más que Ninguna*. Icaria, 1995.

Stone, Alison. "Mother-Daughter Relations and the Maternal in Irigaray and Chodorow." *philoSOPHIA: A Journal of Continental Feminism*, vol. 1, no. 1, 2011, pp. 45-64.

Chapter 4

# Woman-as-Child-to-the-Mother

Joan Garvan

Here is a glimpse of both my mum and of me, the murky ground between mother and daughter, as well as the dynamics within time and place, culture, and society. In this piece, I give an outline of the circumstances surrounding my birth and how I have come to understand the consequent effect on my relationship with my mother. I outline understandings that surfaced after the birth of my first child, and I talk about the outcome in terms of the phrase woman-as-child-to-the-mother. By this I mean given the opportunity to understand and traverse the complexities of birth and mothering—which necessarily include the mother's experience of being mothered—my sense of self as a woman has been renewed.

My mum passed away feeling bitter and cheated. I feel cheated, too—cheated of the love that can be a product of a genuine relationship rather than the cardboard cutout that motherhood, as identity, offers us. My mum was a deserted wife, with two small children, in late-1940s, postwar Australia. There was no money coming in from her first husband, and the regulations that came with the deserted wives' pension were invasive and humiliating. At times, my mother worked three jobs, and it was during this time that my mother met my father. My mum liked my dad well enough, but the marriage was forced on the couple by the pending birth of a child—my birth.

Not long before my mother passed away, it was Christmas time, and my mum had too much to drink. She sat, head in hands saying, "You wouldn't believe the shame." She was talking about the shame she felt being an unmarried and pregnant woman in 1950s Australia. It was devastating. She could not say anymore—and neither could I. My father came from a Catholic family. At the time, there were strict church rules that forbade a Catholic marrying a Protestant, particularly a divorced woman with children. My grandmother, my father's mother, offered my mother money to dissuade her from marrying my father, saying that she would bring me up; nevertheless, my parents tied the knot.

At my mother's eightieth birthday, she reflected on the decades of her life. She remembered wonderful times spent with her father, and a happy childhood, but when she came to the 1950s and the 1960s, when her children were growing up, she described them as "the dark years." Children, for my mother, represented her greatest pain and her greatest joy. But they did not and could not give back to her the person she lost and never found again. She was constrained within the strictures of motherhood.[1]

In 1930s Australia, sex education in schools was nonexistent, and for Catholics in the 1950s, contraception was seen as dubious if not sinful; much later in life, my father confirmed to me that this was his belief, and my mum said she was naive and uninformed in all things sexual. Divorced women and unmarried mothers were shamed, a phenomenon captured by Anne Summers in *Damned Whores and God's Police*.

Married women could be employed in what was considered unskilled positions and their wages were most often half that of men. This was a time of a firm gender divide between the male breadwinner and the female carer, the mother.

After becoming a mother for the first time, I came to think of the legacy of my birth as a broken heart. This may sound overstated or melodramatic to some, but it remains true to me. It may be a consequence of the foundational nature of the connection or the product of a series of unexplained episodes with my mother. My mum gave me clues, tiny fragments of my early life, and I would piece them together bit by bit. And now, I understand my relationship with my mother as a product of circumstances that she did not and could not speak about with me—a new life complicated by factors unknown and unfathomable to a young mind.

I turn to the continuing work that has helped me piece the story together, the way I have come to understand it. Feminist social theorists have brought attention to an essential male centeredness that, in theory, represents masculinity as the norm (Parker; Chodorow, "Reproduction of Mothering"; Hollway, "Capacity to Care"). The case in point is research in psychoanalysis and maternal experience. The infant in physical union with the mother is born and begins the journey to selfhood. Theorists, such as John Bowlby and to a lesser extent Donald Winnicott, have focused on the effect of birth and separation on the child, but what of the mother (Hollway, "Family Figures")?

Jessica Benjamin brought attention to interactions between the mother and her infant as central to infant psychic development, highlighting an inherent struggle for recognition that informs continuing processes of integration and separation. In her work, she attempts to understand the dynamics and sets out to explore the intersubjective realm. The intense physical experience of pregnancy and birth entails both psychological and emotional elements that are carried through into the postnatal phase, which often elicit strong connections with the mother's experience of infancy (Benjamin; Stone). I suggest that my experience of revisiting the circumstances of my birth is indicative of a grappling, a redefining of self—woman-as-child-to-the-mother.

The necessary steps from symbiotic union to separation are not accomplished in the actual birth but are a product of cultural practices that can assist or hamper both mother and baby. Issues related to identity, which many women experience when they become first time mothers, are a product of inadequate understandings—practices that have historically failed to articulate and traverse maternal entanglements.

When a child is born the complex interactions between mother and baby require the mother to renegotiate her sense of self that is separate from her infant while being mindful of the needs and requirements of her baby. She needs to be responsive to her baby but not be overcome by a desire to be everything to the child (Benjamin 88-93). She needs to understand emotional connections and disconnections that may come between this foundational relationship; it is a continuing and unfolding process. For the new mother, this includes revisiting the connection with one's mother from a new and different perspective (Stone).

How do these understandings relate to my story? The way I see it is that my mum understandably carried with her mixed and perhaps tumultuous feelings about my birth. She was never able to explore all this complexity; after all, there were three more babies to come, and what of the first two? My mum and I were never able to talk about the circumstances, or resolve the feelings, related to the pregnancy, the consequent marriage, and the life that followed, although they are necessarily linked. I was forty-two when my first baby came along. This was not simply an outcome of my early life; however, the decision to have a child was intense. I went on to think of my relationship with my two children as complicated by factors I did not understand. Nancy Chodorow's notion of shadow feelings captured something I felt compelled to explore. There were times when my first was young and I had some time to myself that I felt frozen on where to turn next. I was plagued with questions that began to be quelled by research on the experience of women as mothers.

The last days of my mother's life were a whirl of emotions, but on the day my mother died, the last person she called for was my dad and the last name she said was mine— perhaps, in those last hours, this was all that was needed. Entanglements between mothers and their children may always be complex, but we will hopefully find better ways to explain and facilitate connections along with disconnections that accommodate the needs of both mother and child. Ambivalence can lead us to explore and possibly understand more fully emotional worlds. Woman-as-child-to-the-mother— I now have an understanding of the constraints and complexities of motherhood so that I can get on with mothering.

## Endnotes

1. I am drawing here from Adrienne Rich's distinction between motherhood, which is the social structuring of care for infants and children, which is gendered and privatized within the family, and mothering, the everyday practice of care. Constraints are prescriptions for what it means to be a good mother and include taboos about expressing any ambivalences women may hold about their children or their new social location (Parker; Garvan).

## Works Cited

Benjamin, J. *Like Subject, Love Object: Essays on Recognition and Sexual Difference.* Yale University Press. 1995.

Chodorow, Nancy. *The Reproduction of Mothering: Psychoanalysis and Sociology of Gender.* University of California Press. 1978.

Chodorow, Nancy. *The Power of Feelings: Personal Meaning in Psychoanalysis, Gender, and Culture.* Yale University Press, 1999.

Garvan, Joan. *Maternal Ambivalence in Contemporary Australia: Navigating Equity and Care.* Dissertation. Australian National University, 2010.

Hollway, Wendy. "Family Figures in 20th Century British 'Psy' Discourse". *Theory and Psychology.* 16 (4). 2006. 443-64.

Hollway, Wendy. *The Capacity to Care: Gender and Ethical Subjectivity.* Routledge, 2006.

Parker, Rozsika. *Torn in Two: The Experience of Maternal Ambivalence.* Virago, 2005.

Rich, Adrienne. *Of Woman Born: Motherhood as Experience and Institution.* Virago Books, 1986.

Stone, Alison. *Feminism, Psychoanalysis, and Maternal Subjectivity.* Routledge, 2011.

Summers, Anne. *Damned Whores and God's Police: The Colonization of Women in Australia.* Penguin, 1975.

Chapter 5

# Mother of Mother of Mother

Andi Spark

# mother of mother of mother

Mother's house had a grand sweeping entrance hall staircase a 'la Tara.

Such an incongruous woman;
part southern belle (Aus style) part practical ex-tomboy.
Vastly different,
yet my daughter posed so many echoes of my mother.

**Worlds collided.**

She only slept in straight-up deadman position – the silk pillowcase ensuring perfectly coiffed hair that would last the week.

Always immaculately dressed, even her dressing gown conveyed a faux-regal demeanour.

Her old school cut-crystal dresser tray was a childhood fascination ... harkening to aristocratic roots

...and the silverplate hairbrush that left multiple wicked bruises on my bum

I think often about expectations...

...and how I could never live up to my Mother's expectations

Our school motto:

I was a high achiever at high school - awarded colours every year. And every year my blazer pocket got bigger to accommodate them all. By the end, even the embroidery company expected me to be the House Captain. But I wasn't chosen.

## I'd long internalized disappointment.

the winning tree   my 3rd place

Where I grew up, we celebrated Arbor Day with a tree planting ceremony. And an art competition. In year 4, I lost* to a ridiculously naff lollipop drawing.

I vowed to never enter a competition again.

*the judges thought that someone else had drawn my entry
- a proper artist maybe

## I always felt so misinterpreted

I worked tirelessly for more than a year on a feature film project about a little girl who won't/can't speak, that turns into a curlew —a metaphoric magic realist fable about voicelessness and destruction of habitat.

It was an exquisite extravaganza of entirely hand-painted animation. Every week during our phonecalls I updated her on the trials and pains of bringing such a labour-intensive production to screen. She couldn't wait to see it.

Finally, when I showed her the VHS, she 'switched' off

less than ten minutes into it...

And yet, she once told me she was
jealous of my choices – how I could
live the *sex drugs rock n roll life
(*this wasn't really acceptable mind you)
– but mainly I would choose Art;
choose a life and career where I could
use my talents
(even if they weren't what she expected)

Someone said to me 'You Reap What You Sow'

What did that actually mean?!

← wooden spoon
← stick
← brush
← anything to hand

She was unbelievably strict
Obsessed with order and control
She never hugged us;
never said she loved us;
never let herself soften.

She wasn't the mummy I wanted

Nor the mother I wanted to be

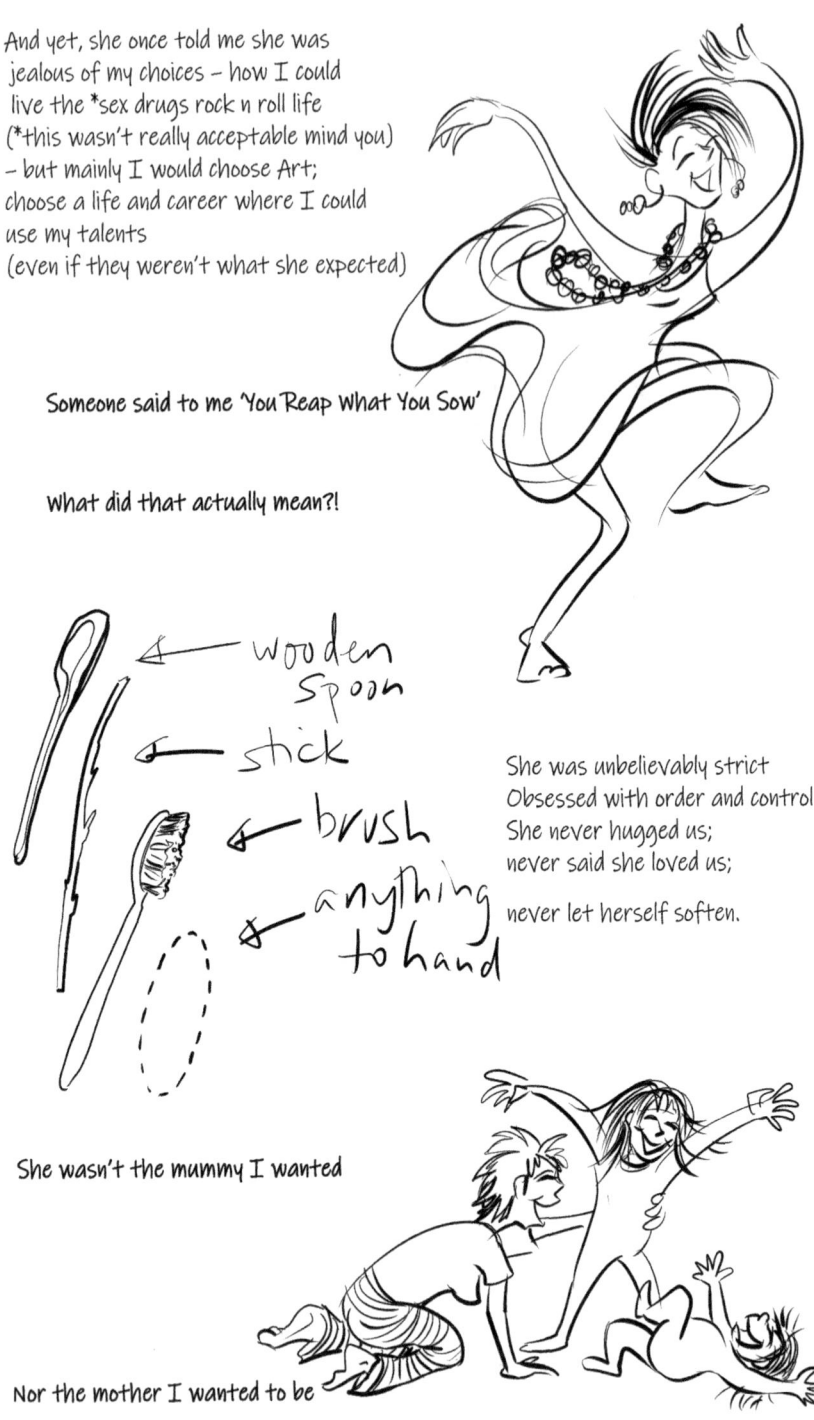

## Obsessiveness runs in our blood

My daughter wore her god-sisters hand-me-down dress Every day until it literally rotted off her.

age three  age five  age seven

Perseverance and Preservation
are deeply rooted in both their characters

## Mother's Shoe Collection Was Legendary

"Pinch the heels"

She was vigilant in always
squeezing the back of the heels
to keep them tight and in shape.

Sloppy shoes = slovenly morals

Stored in original boxes:
coded by colour; season; style;
and coordinated with every outfit

Mother had her hair done in elaborate Rococo styles every Friday —backcombed and teased amidst whorls of hairspray.

My teen daughter was also obsessed with hair-dos.

And spray.

# And then the unexpected happens

At the moment my mother became hospitalized forever,
my teenage daughter gave birth.

"The heart of a mother is a deep abyss
at the bottom of which
you will always find forgiveness"

(Honore de Balzac 1799 – 1850)

# MOTHER OF MOTHER OF MOTHER

I am equally horrified and fascinated.
Shocked into ghastly recognition of this generational cataclysm

## correlations were abundant

The baby constantly lined up his cars, classified by size.. colour.. type...

Mother used to line up the Moccona "pantry" on the kitchen bench.
Precisely.

It reminds me of my daughters seminal period of shaved eyebrows.
It was all about...

# ORDER & CONTROL

And me?
Was there something about being an animator that spoke to obsession with minutiae and detail? Repetitive and precise.

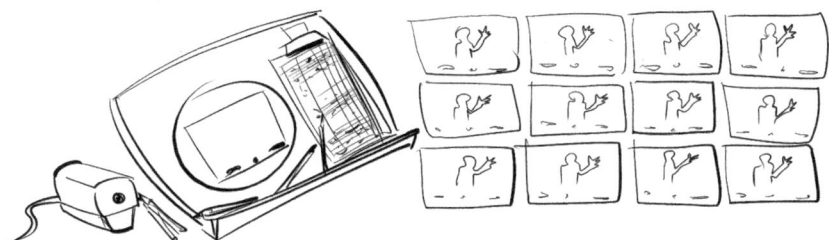

Yet my mother's rages were uncontrolled
and my daughter was uncontrollable.
Everything was spiralling out of my control.

Mother's diagnosis is terminal.
A long slow decline to death.
My failurefeeling is cloying.

Mother always said that she didn't like "people" only little babies and the very elderly. (I figured it was because they can't answer back.)

Propped up in the hospital bed, the baby shared his bottle with her like he knew she was sick and needed sustenance.

She went along with the game with unrecognisable playfulness.

**Her disease progressed.**
Just as we finished having to feed the baby puree, mother went from "solids" to jellies

Is it guilt?
Assuaging my guilt?

By looking after the invalid and the baby I am somehow looking after the daughter I had failed, and

the daughter I'd failed to be.

## Finding words / Losing words

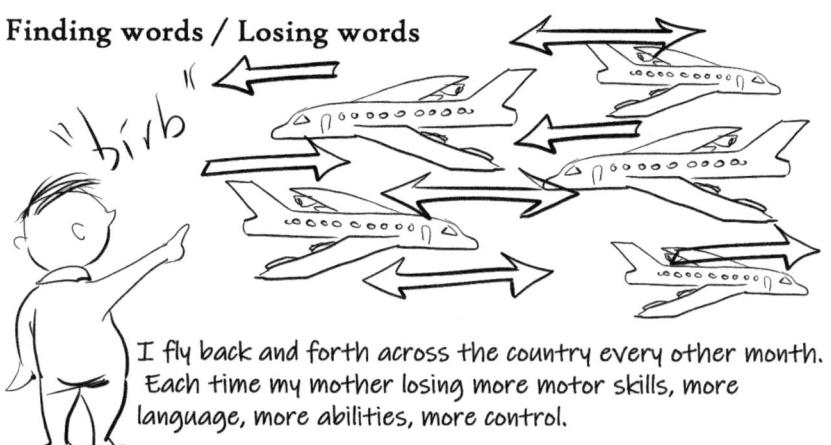

I fly back and forth across the country every other month. Each time my mother losing more motor skills, more language, more abilities, more control.

(Our house is under a flight path)

I am surrounded by the rage of people being misunderstood: the toddler; the teenager; the terminally ill.

I wipe my mother's bottom, her snot, dabbing her spittle, her spilt food as if I can earn some god points or something. Hypocritical and poignant at the same time.

Who am I doing this for? Her? Me? Some act of contrition? as penance for hating her? Will I be absolved? Will she?

Have we reached the bottom of the abyss yet?

I arrive one day to find her in a frenzy, pulling and yanking at her underwear.

But she can no longer speak. Just make inarticulate shouty sounds. The irony of this is ridiculous.

All her life she's worn glorious French-style silk and lace matching cami/knickers/slip sets. Despite being relegated to nappies and body-length bibs, every day she insists on getting dressed for no one in her fancy underwear. The nurses and orderlies do their best to give her a semblance of dignity.

She's crying (but she can't actually cry anymore thanks to the cruel illness.)

## Finally it clicked: "same same but different"

To the untrained eye, the lace on the pink lace cami and the pink lace slip look the same.
Only I could know the difference.
Maybe this was my absolution. My true purpose. Travelling an eight thousand kilometer round trip as often as possible to ensure she has matching underwear.
And only me, having grown up intimately absorbing her order and control; the one person in the world who could understand her; could live up to her expectations.

The last time I saw her was a shock by anyone's reckoning

No longer even able to hold up her head, her crippled hands still grasped the bear I'd given her a few years before that never once left her side (like I'd had to.)

the "Me" bear →

← old threadbare bear

The "me" bear was a companion to "old threadbare bear" who'd sat sentinel on her (immaculately made) bed every day of her life at home
—a stoic symbol for something I never understood.

When she finally died, we organised for an open casket.
I needed to hug her one last time.
To give her all the tenderness and caring
and mothering that she had so desperately needed all her life.

And forgiveness.

I'd taken the "favourite" old and cracked up wooden spoon to bury with her.

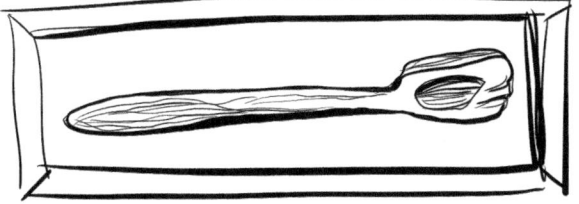

In the end I kept it.

But both the bears went with her.

Chapter 6

# Becoming a Mother Philosopher

Cassie Premo Steele

> And now, since I have taught that things cannot be born from nothing, nor the same, when born, to nothing be recalled, doubt not my words.
>
> —Lucretius, *On the Nature of Things*, 50 BCE

I grew up in the house of a philosopher mother. So like Lucretius, I knew that I was not born from nothing, yet it seemed to me that my difference from her was so profound that I sometimes doubted my own existence.

She was a thinker. I was a feeler. She was loud. I was quiet. She expressed anger. I showed mostly fear.

In my mind, there existed an ideal mother. She was not hard to imagine. I saw them everywhere—at school, at church, in the neighbourhood. She did not have a job. She baked cookies and stayed home. She loved her husband. She was not a philosopher.

Five hundred years before Lucretius, a philosopher named Thales posited that everything was made from one substance. He looked at water—in rain, in snow and ice, in steam and river—and decided that despite the changing nature of the universe, all is one.

A lifetime later, I would apply these questions to myself. How does a mother give birth to a daughter so very different from herself yet still be of the same origin? How does a married mother at midlife give birth to a lesbian self so very different from who she had been yet still be herself? And what does philosophy have to do with it all?

It had been years since my mother came to my house when my husband was not home. We had hosted her for birthdays—hers, my stepfather's, mine, my husband's, my daughter's—and for Thanksgiving, for Christmas and New Year's dinners, as well as for Easter, along with ordinary Sundays of sandwiches, crudités, and wine.

But this day was different. On this day, my mother was coming to the house so I could tell her the reason my husband was not home was that the week before, I told him I was gay.

Like Lucretius and Thales before him, Pythagoras saw a unified pattern in the world. Where Lucretius saw primal germs and Thales saw water, Pythagoras saw triangles. While ancient farmers used his theorem to plot the corners of their fields along the Nile every year, Pythagoras saw these right angles extending indefinitely to the spheres that revolved around the earth and made music as they turned.

The triangles of Nazi Germany. The triangles of gay pride. The triangles of my mother and father and me, my sister and mother and me, my mother and daughter and me.

My earliest memory of my mother was the hard-skinned table of her pregnant belly, with my sister in it, as my mother flipped through index cards of numbers and quizzed me.

The card said thirteen.

I knew that one. It was the number of my birthday. But I pretended not to know.

"What do you mean, you don't know?" she said, exasperated at me. Like Aristotle, she believed all potentiality is held within us from birth, like an acorn holds the potentiality of an ancient oak tree.

I was two-and-a-half years old.

Muggy wind wheezed through the window. She wiped her forehead. I know now, as a mother, just how pregnancy turns a woman's body into an incubator. It was August in Milwaukee, Wisconsin. My sister would be born in two weeks.

We both looked towards the window, maybe in an attempt to will more air through. Instead, we saw my father walk away.

I knew where he was going. He was going to the shrink. I knew this because I have heard them arguing. He goes to the shrink, and it does not help. He is still an asshole.

My mother whipped her head back towards me. "You know this number," she snapped. "I know you do."

I did. She was right. She was always right. She was super smart, my mom. The other moms sat around on park benches with their kids during the day, but my mom went to graduate school. She hired a nice fat Russian woman named Mary to sit around on park benches with me. Mary always had food in her bag—chips and a thermos filled with chocolate milk. She made my favourite food for lunch—hot dogs and baked beans, which she called "beans and wieners." Mary did not do the number cards with me.

"What is it?" my mother growled.

"Thirteen," I sighed.

"Yes. God. Finally," she said, and started to put the flash cards away.

This is why I pretended not to know the answer: I knew that thirteen was the last number in the pack. The only one we had not done. I knew that once I answered that one, she would put the cards away. The lesson would be over. She would be done with me for the day.

You could not step into the same river twice, famously said Heraclitus, a philosopher from the fifth century BCE. Heraclitus also believed in the "upward-downward path," by which he meant that one transformation was balanced by its opposite.

I always knew I was different from the person my parents thought I was born to be.

I changed my name at the age of three. Until that time, my babysitter, Mary, had the same name as I did: Mary. My birth name is Mary.

My aunt's name was Mary, too. I was born at Saint Joseph's Hospital, and you know the name of His wife.

So many Marys! A river of Marys! I could not stand to step into another one!

Here is what I did: I waited until my mother was getting dressed to go out. She was busy. She was rushed. She was distracted. It was a perfect setting for my announcement.

My mother was sitting at a makeup table looking in the mirror, wearing a long orange maxi dress (it was 1970; they were everywhere), and I walked into the room and said, "Do not call me Mary anymore.

From now on, my name is Cassie."

She looked at me. She held her clip-on earring an inch away from her ear, as if in a still-frame painting, and she said nothing.

No argument. No admonition. No dismissal.

From that moment in 1970 and for the rest of my life, people have called me Cassie. It is my name. It is who I am. Hardly anyone knows that my birth name is Mary. It feels like another person to me. I feel like if I had stayed Mary, I would still be in the Midwest, would have married a Catholic man, would still go to church regularly, and might occasionally vote Republican.

What is a name anyway? An illusion? A marker, a pointer, an arrow heading towards the vast unknowable self that changes and grows and holds constancy only in change?

This sounds like a very postmodern notion, but actually, it is ancient.

Parmenides, who lived at the same time as Socrates and Plato, thought everything was, at essence, both an illusion and a constant. By applying logic to his understanding, he concluded that

1. Things cannot exist and not exist at the same time.
2. Things cannot come from nothing.
3. The world has always existed.
4. Change is an illusion.
5. Existence is a hidden constant.

My wife once asked me how I came up with the name Cassie.

"It came from a song my parents used to sing to me," I said. "When they would change my diaper, my parents would sing, 'Kissy Cass, another lass. Kissie Cassie, another lassie.'"

"Were you still in diapers at the age of three when you changed your name?" she asked.

"No," I said. "I don't think so."

"So, you remembered the song they sang to you as a baby when they changed your diapers?" she asked. "How is that possible?"

I shrugged. "I don't know. It just is."

She let it go. She loves me because of my stories.

But maybe the story is an illusion, yet somehow here I am, with this new name.

Over the years, I come to claim the meaning of my name:

Cassandra, from ancient Greek mythology, was given the gift of prophecy from the god Apollo, but when she refused to lie down with him, he cursed her so that no one would believe what she said.

My mother would have never named me Cassandra. It is pagan. It is not from the Bible.

Yet still I become like Cassandra. The one who remembers. The one who tells the truth. Even when the truth is changing.

In Nepal, ten years before Pythagoras and a hundred years before Parmenides, a man named Siddhartha Gautama was born, who would become known as Buddha. He came to the conclusion, after much suffering and witnessing of suffering, that the truth of existence is suffering and that our desire to do away with suffering only leads to more. The trick to escaping this loop is to abandon desire.

I had a bit of the Bodhi tree experience myself at the age of nine.

My parents had divorced the year before, and my mom was attending a philosophy seminar at Haverford, a men's college outside Philadelphia. My sister and I came with her, but she stayed in her own dorm room, across the hall.

My sister slept in a narrow bed across the room from me, and our mother's room was across the hall. We ate at the college cafeteria for lunch without our mom. We filled up on chocolate pudding and red jello. We were mostly on our own.

I was not scared. Not of being alone, anyway. I was afraid of my toes.

My sister and I would spend all day at the college pool, running around barefoot, and by this point halfway through the summer, the bottoms of my feet looked like shredded cheese.

At night, the stiffly bleached sheets provided by the college caught and pulled on the skin of my toes, ripping the flesh, so I woke in a flash of pain in the dark room and felt the warm blood pooling onto the white cotton.

One night, I decided I was tired of getting bled to death without adult supervision, and so I woke my sister and said, "We're going to go get Mom."

We ventured out into the hallway. It was long and brightly lit even in the middle of the night and carpeted industrial red. We knocked, tentatively, on her door across the hall, knowing it was not really her door. It opened, like ours did, into a suite that she shared with a roommate.

The door opened. A woman with glasses and a book in her hands looked at us.

"She's not here," she said. "She went to a party. Room 301."

We nodded and walked away.

301 was one floor up. Our friends Alex and Alicia stayed on that floor with their parents. They were from California and they loved the rainy weather we had here. It is always sunny in California, they said. The Philadelphia rain was better. They were so sick of the sun.

I thought about this as we walked up the stairs towards the third floor. How can a person get sick of the sun? When we left Philadelphia at the end of the summer, we would go home to Minnesota, where the leaves would start falling by August. Snow would come by September. Snow was something I could imagine getting sick of. Not the sun. This was a revelation to me, perhaps my first philosophical thought, at the age of nine, that even something as wonderful as the sun can become a negative presence in the right circumstance.

We walked to the end of the third-floor hallway, and there it was: 301.

My sister and I looked at each other. She said nothing. I knew it was up to me to knock. So I did.

The door opened, and there, sitting on a table, being held up by six men from the seminar, philosophy professors like my mother, was my mother.

They all looked at us simultaneously.

"Look, girls!" one of them yelled. "It worked! We're holding her up with just one finger each!"

I zoomed in to their hands and saw, indeed, that each man was using just one index finger to hold up the table, which was, in turn, holding our mother.

Of course it worked. Of course she was on a table. Of course this was fun. Of course we were bothering her.

How could a bleeding big toe in the middle of the night possibly compete with this circus show starring my mother?

"What do you want?" she asked, the table wobbling beneath her.

"Nothing," I said, already backing away. "Just wanted to see where you were. Have fun."

And as we walked down the concrete steps back to our dorm room, I thought my second philosophical thought of my life—that even something as wonderful as a fun mom can be not so much fun, given the right circumstance.

In other words, it is all suffering. It just takes different shapes depending on perspective.

When my mother arrived at the house on the day I came out to her as a lesbian, she brought presents—a week-old chocolate Easter bunny for Lily and a birthday present for me because my birthday was a week away.

She handed me a small, wrapped box. I opened it. It was a ring. A silver ring with a square moonstone that looked like a diamond. It looked like an engagement ring.

"I love it!" I said to her. "It's the best present I've ever gotten!"

Her eyebrows went up. I had rejected so many of her presents in the past—embroidered tops, yellow sweaters, outfits that felt too Talbot's and not enough Chico's for me.

"Look inside," she said. "It's engraved."

I held the ring to the light. I was turning forty six in a week, and I needed new glasses. Inside was my name and my birth date: Cassie, April thirteen.

It is an engagement ring, I thought. I am getting married to myself.

I thanked and hugged her and told her it was the best present she had ever given me. She was not used to this kind of acceptance from me.

So she said, "Okay, what's going on?"

Instead of using words, I held out my left hand to her and showed her my ring finger, ringless, with three red lines engraved in the skin where my wedding and engagement rings used to be.

I looked into her eyes. She understood right away.

"What happened?" she asked.

"I am gay," I said.

And then she said, "This will be a fight. You will have to get a lawyer. You will have to learn to fight."

"I don't want to fight with him," I said.

"I know you feel that way. I remember when I was divorcing your father, and I called my dad to tell him that he was suing me for alimony. You could have heard him screaming from Detroit to Minnesota even if there had been no phone."

I was amazed that she was so very allied with me in this—that everything I said to her, she paralleled with an experience of her own. Empathy. I felt as if I had fallen into a rabbit hole of mother love. What I always longed for and felt I would never have.

Later, we went out to the yard to play with the dog. My mom had her arm cocked in the air and threw the yellow ball to her dog who was poised to chase it with doglike enthusiasm.

Then she paused and said, "This is the best day of my life."

"Really?" I asked, still reeling from the support I was getting from her.

The dog bounded across the yard, where over the past five years I had planted roses and vegetables and lilies and a pomegranate tree. My mother said, "Yes. My Cassie is a grown woman. And she is standing up for herself."

"One is not born but becomes a woman," wrote Simone de Beauvoir. Gone was the Mary I was born to be: quiet, fearful, and overflowing with feeling. In coming out to my mother as a mother at midlife, I stepped into the river of becoming a mother philosopher: standing up for who she wanted to be.

"Doubt not my words," I heard the echo of Lucretius in my head as my mother's dog joyfully brought her ball back to me.

Chapter 7

# "Get Something in Your Head, and They Can't Take It Away": Education as a Family Value Passed through Black Mississippi Mothers

Marcia Allen Owens

Drawing on experiences, as well as family and community history, the following narrative presents an account of the intersections of race, gender, and family concerning education and development. My story is autobiographical, biographical, and historical. It is autobiographical in that I share a closeup vision of my lived experience from childhood to my present career but biographical in that the stories of my grandmother and mother profoundly inform and influence mine. Finally, this narrative is historical in that I chronicle my lived experience of desegregation in the post-Brown era as well as in the academy.

My grandmother's foundation and my mother's strong guidance pushed me into a science, technology, engineering, and mathematics (STEM) career, and I am a second-generation professor at a historically Black college and university (HBCU). Calling herself a quasi-feminist, I watched my mother navigate the racism, sexism, and misogynoir of the Jim Crow South, the civil rights movement and higher education, to become the first woman College vice-president in the state of Mississippi. Once I became a mother myself, the wisdom of my grandmother, passed on through my own mother, was an ever-present force navigating motherhood and career. The perfect storm of maternal knowledge, wisdom, access, courage, and resilience prevailed to transmit the foundational value of education for two (and counting) generations of formal educational opportunities in an unlikely location and in dangerous times.

## Grenada, Mississippi, in Context

The landmark decision of the US Supreme Court in *Brown v. Board of Education* was handed down in 1954, yet the first Mississippi public school was not desegregated until August 31, 1964. Ten of the state's nearly two hundred districts had resisted desegregation to the point that all federal funds had been terminated; Grenada County was among this group (Leeson).

Implementation of freedom of choice, which was forced by the federal lawsuit *Cunningham et al. v. Grenada Municipal Separate School District*, was the focus of Dr. Martin Luther King Jr.'s last visit to Grenada. At the age of five, this was the only time that I was allowed to attend a march during the King years. As a result of legal action, Grenada reluctantly acquiesced and implemented a freedom of choice plan. On the first morning of the fall term of 1966, three hundred Black students had registered and 150 actually showed up to attend Grenada's previously all-White Lizzie Horn Elementary and John Rundle High schools, and the resulting violence was reported in *Time*, *Newsweek*, and *US News and World Report*.

Court-ordered desegregation was implemented on March 16, 1970, resulting in a sudden spring break transition to desegregated schools. After spring break, I became the only Black child in my class. Grenada's desegregation efforts honoured the letter of the law but certainly not its spirit. Their plan was to have a school within a school. All of the Black children at the newly integrated Lizzie Horn Elementary School were placed in the lower sections. Initially, no Black children were in Section 4-1. Racial segregation, school officials contended, was merely coincidental, and the school had placed me in the top Black section, maybe 4-6 or 4-7; however, my activist educator parents knew that standardized test scores were the justification for tracking. Therefore, my parents met with the principal, arguing that my scores were in the ninety-eighth percentile. Even though there were other Black children who had scores high enough to be in the upper sections, for various reasons, their parents did not press the case.

## Tracking and Gifted Education

Academic ability grouping practices were outcomes of *Brown* and led to tracking students according to standardized tests, which presumably measure intelligence (Donelan, Neal, and Jones). Grenada Municipal Separate School District used the California Achievement Test, grouping students according to their reading score, and resulted in all-white classes and all Black classes; essentially two schools within a school.

The advent of gifted education in Mississippi closely paralleled the end of segregated schools, and in 1973, gifted education was included in the Mississippi state law. In 1974, Mississippi adopted the 1972 federal definition of gifted and talented children, as those "by virtue of outstanding abilities are capable of high performance" in areas of 1) general intellectual ability, 2) specific academic aptitude, 3) creative or productive thinking, 4) leadership ability, 5) visual and performing arts, and/or 6) psychomotor ability (Karnes and Collins 45).

Even now, gifted education models still "lack an appreciation of the abilities of Black girls to navigate different cultural environments—the White dominated school environment, the male dominated social practices, and their own cultural communities" (Evans-Winters 26).

## Early Life

My father, Willie T. Allen, was principal of Holcomb Colored Elementary School (later named Rebecca Reed Elementary) located ten miles west of the county seat of Grenada. Holcomb Colored Elementary was a "Brown" school, built in 1954. He described these schools in a 1997 interview: "The school, schools all over Mississippi were built out of cinder blocks, and they got so popular after the *Brown* decision, they called them "Nigger Blocks".... They built them in a hurry over the next ten or twelve years, to try to keep from integrating" (Personal interview).

At three, I started going to school with my daddy. I had my own schedule. I began each school day in first grade spending time with Mrs. Springfield and third grade with Mrs. Knox. I then went to the cafeteria to butter the yeast rolls with Mrs. Sweezer and Mrs. Bryant. I then went to eighth grade with Mrs. Hardiman and ended each day working in the principal's office with Mrs. Golliday. I was constantly learning and nicknamed the "School Baby."

By the time I was six, as there was no kindergarten, I began first grade in town at the all-Black Willia Wilson Elementary. I was gifted, but gifted programs did not yet exist, so after only two weeks in first grade, I was moved to the second grade. I finished my work and disrupted the teacher by helping everyone else with their work.

In my now-adult estimation, I was not socially prepared for the move. They told me that I was going to the second grade because the first grade class was crowded. However, it did not click until much later that I was the only one who had moved. When I went to second grade, I promptly won the spelling bee, with the word "grapes." This was probably my first lesson in resilience because all the other second graders except lifelong friend Audrey House, were angry that this little girl who just got here came in and won the spelling bee.

## Generations of Gifted Girls

Mary Montie proposes that gifted children often have gifted parents (22). Although genetics may play a role, this is, however, confounded by the environment. Environmental factors, such as birthplace and upbringing, in addition to social, political, and economic influences, have an impact and serve to enhance individual attributes. Accordingly, my mother would have also likely been labelled gifted, as she also read at an early age due to the teaching of her older sister, Henri Marie Brown. Similarly, my mother skipped not one, but two grades.

My mother grew up in poverty during the Jim Crow era in Grenada, Mississippi, with a father and mother who had fourth and seventh grade educations, respectively. Even in poverty, however, my maternal grandmother had a vision for a better future for her children and a profound value for education. As family legend heralds, my grandmother, Jessye Weeks Jones (who died before I turned two), agreed to marry my grandfather, Ben Jones, if he promised that he would move "to town" once their first child reached school age. Rural schools were scheduled according to agricultural seasons and children were also labourers. Moving to town meant that they could attend nine-month schools. My grandfather honoured his promise and the two of them, with much criticism from family and community, put four of their five children through college in Mississippi during the 1950s.

As the second youngest child, my mother, Mildred, was actually the first to graduate college. Her older sister was already a teacher because a college degree was not yet required to teach Black students; for her, the family value of education was her movement:

> I realized that if I remained in Grenada without an education, the only job that I could have were the jobs where I could cook in greasy spoons ... or work in one of those white homes as a domestic worker or a keeper of their children. That's when my movement started because I did not want to do that.... My movement started in terms of the building of self-image, and I think that's where it must start if it's going to have the most permanent effect for people. These things I did—like challenging a city court in 1957 in Grenada, Mississippi—were just natural; it had to come out. When you make your mind up that you're going to be something, that you're going to lift yourself from certain circumstances, that's the beginning of your movement. (Personal interview)

Thus, I am at least the third generation of gifted girls.

## A Lost Value of Segregated Schools

My mother went on to graduate as valedictorian of her class in 1950. As was the practice, she received valedictory scholarships to all five of Mississippi's historically Black colleges and universities. Her choice was both guided and limited by knowledge, accessibility, and another painful remnant of history. The state capital of Jackson was accessible from Grenada by train so her choices were Jackson College for Negro Teachers (now Jackson State University) and Tougaloo College. However, the intraracial mores of the day included colourism, and she was too dark skinned to attend Tougaloo, so she enrolled at Jackson College for Negro Teachers, where she majored in language arts. After graduating with honors in 1954, she returned home to Grenada to teach in a one-room school where many of the students were older.

Since their career options were severely limited this meant that all-Black schools were staffed by teachers who were the best and brightest that the Black community had to offer. Another advantage was that they were part of the community; they went to church with us and knew students and their families outside of the classroom. Although they shared the same burdens of racism indicative of time and place, teachers were revered, respected, and influential community leaders. With limited material resources, our teachers cultivated each student's gifts, even though students of varying abilities were in the same classes.

## My Experience of Desegregation in Grenada

My fourth grade year began my personal experience with the intersection of race and gender. I knew about many of my parents' struggles, but I had been sheltered and protected from the individual impact and microaggressions well before the term was coined. I had heard the adage and instruction, "You have to work twice as hard to get half of what they get." Once I entered the classroom alone, there were several explicit and implicit amendments. You may work twice as hard, but you still might not get what you earned or deserve. It seemed unfair. Desegregation resulted in my own interpretations. Initially, I thought that the proverbial "they" was White people, but it was also applicable to inequities at the hands of and for the benefit of Black boys and men: "You may work twice as hard, but don't embarrass the boys." But the louder voice was that of my mother: "There's nothing that a dumb man can do for you" or "I'll follow a man, but he has to be going somewhere."

My experiences in fourth and fifth grades were a test of my resilience and the place of some significant "firsts." It was the first time that I was called "nigger" to my face. It was also the first time that I was called "stupid." It was the first time that I was assigned a grade lower than an A, and it was the first time that I was called "dumb." Thankfully, I had a firm foundation because I knew for certain, even in fourth grade, that I was not dumb, even when "dumb" served as a modifying descriptor of the racist slur "nigger."

The effects of classroom racism are lasting; however, resilience runs parallel (Housee and Richards). Through teaching an ethics of justice, community, and care, my mother modelled and equipped me to face, confront, and endure intersectional injustices as a Black girl in the American South.

## The University of Mississippi

During the height of the Civil Rights Movement, my mother began her master's degree at the University of Mississippi and was scheduled to graduate in 1971. In the summer of the same year, she was approached to work on her doctorate, less than ten years after the first Black student had been admitted to the institution. Initially, however, she refused, so as to honor traditional gender roles:

> They asked me to come back and work on my doctorate. I said, "why me?" They said they had looked at my GRE scores and at my record. I said I cannot do that. My husband believes that the man should take care of the family. He would tell me to go on, but I know the bills that we have made were contingent upon two salaries coming into the house. (Personal interview)

Nevertheless, after more civil unrest in Grenada, my mother resigned and started her doctoral studies in educational psychology at the University of Mississippi.

During her coursework phase, I would ride the fifty-two miles from Grenada to Oxford, Mississippi, with my mother. Most of the time, I would sit in on her classes or just outside the door, reading and listening. But one day, she said that I was going to be part of her class presentation. During her class, I sat for a test in another room, which I later learned was the Stanford Binet Intelligence Test. The following week, she dressed me in my favourite short set and sandals, and I sat before the class, read for them, and answered their questions. I did not understand why they were so impressed by me reading and talking to them, but I now know that for some, gifted Black women and girls are always the exception, yet we refuse to live down to low expectations.

## The Move to Jackson

When my mother finished her coursework and preliminary examinations, she reapplied for a position in the Grenada public schools. That was the first but certainly not the last time that I heard the term "overqualified." However, she was offered a job at Jackson State College, 117 miles away from Grenada. My brother was finishing his junior year of high school, and I was finishing sixth grade. Because of his American College Test (ACT) scores, Michael was offered early admission to Jackson State. So while my father remained in Grenada for ten more years, the three of us moved to Jackson, where my mother took a position in the Counselling Centre.

## STEM Victories and Defeats

By this time, gifted classes were considered advanced in junior high and high school, and I was consistently placed in these classes. I knew that I wanted to major in psychology and go to law school; however, my favourite junior high guidance counsellor projected her own daughter's issues onto my career goals. The counsellor's daughter had majored in psychology and began to have mental health issues because she began to psychoanalyze herself. My mother's goal for me was medical school. In a Black community where teachers were part of the upper echelon, being a medical doctor represented the pinnacle of professional accomplishment. So, I took every advanced science and math class in junior high and high school. I did summer science camps every summer at Jackson State or University of Mississippi Medical Centre. My junior year ACT scores were high enough to warrant an offer of early admission to Jackson State and recruitment to many other institutions, yet I declined, as I was looking forward to my senior year, and I would have entered college at the age of fifteen.

After narrowing down my choices to Vassar, Wellesley, Northwestern, and Jackson State, I decided to attend Jackson State. Having literally grown up on the campus of what was now Jackson State University, I became the fourth member of my family to attend. Graduating with honors in biology with a minor in math, I enjoyed curricular and extracurricular life at my HBCU, along with the overall nurturing environment. Up to this day, HBCUs play a major role in producing Black STEM graduates (Upton and Tennenbaum).

Sexism, misogyny, misogynoir, language, innuendo, and outright advances were prevalent in my undergraduate STEM studies at Jackson State. They were certainly there, but so was my mother, and she was a force to be reckoned with. However, not gaining admission to medical school was my first academic failure, one of epic proportions, since I felt my mother had been disappointed. I applied for postbaccalaureate programs and even pursued a master's in biology to increase my chance of admission. At that point, my mother's dream for me had become my nightmare, as I was engulfed by another academic failure. Never telling my parents the reason why, I decided to walk away from the program without finishing my thesis. I now realize that I was not equipped for failure. Black girls are socialized to be strong enough to handle it, whatever "it" is, because no one is likely to fight against the myriad "it's" that will happen to Black girls.

With the wisdom and examples of my mother and grandmother, I entered Emory School of Law. Although I stepped out on my own, their lessons, values, and resilience spurred me on. Determined to make lemonade from my figurative bushel of lemons, I took the Law School Admissions Test (LSAT) as a walk in, without any preparation. Ironically, reacquainting myself with my own dream led to admission to several law schools, but I chose to stay in Atlanta and attend Emory.

The lessons of Grenada, Mississippi, were instructive throughout law school and my legal career. While practicing law, I entered the family tradition of education by teaching as an adjunct at Emory. By this time, I was married with a family, and the engrained gender norms modelled by my mother influenced me to find a way but not at the expense of my family. So, I enrolled in a PhD program at Emory while practicing law full time. Despite my exhaustion and in the face of myriad challenges, I had a high GPA.

A gifted Black girl with a JD and a PhD brought out the chorus of family and friends chanting, "You're just a professional student," "You just don't want to work," and "Mama taught us to be lifelong learners, but you took her literally." But I had an encounter with God and went on to earn a master of divinity degree (from Emory) where my thesis had a STEM-related focus on environmental justice in the Black Church.

At her retirement in 1999, my mother, Dr. Mildred Jones Allen, had ascended to the level of executive vice president of Jackson State University and became the first woman VP of any race in a state university in Mississippi. My grandmother had planted the seeds of education as a family value, as a key to access and dignity. Repeated by my mother and now me was the saying "Get something in your head, and they can't take it away" (Personal interview). Now, as a second-generation HBCU professor, I live the adage "the more things change, the more they stay the same." I had my mother as a role model of coping, resisting, and resilience. My experiences with patriarchy, microaggressions, and misogynoir as a Black woman STEM professor at an HBCU have been chronicled in other writings (Owens, "Closet Chair and Committee Side Piece"; Owens, "Is That Healthy?"). The skills passed down from my grandmother to my mother and to me, of negotiating oppressive spaces and countering stereotypes, are part of my explicit curriculum. Although I have no daughters of my own, I intentionally take on Black women doctoral students and transmit the knowledge and wisdom and strategies to thrive, not merely survive, that have been passed down for generations. As my grandmother was for her yet unborn children, as my mother was for me and countless others, I am a gifted, fierce, and fearless advocate for my students and many others.

## Works Cited

Anonymous. "Civil Rights: What Grenadans Are Like." *Newsweek*, 26 Sept. 1966, pp. 33-34.

Anonymous. "Mississippi: Grenada Revisited." *Newsweek*, 25 July 1966, pp. 29-30.

Anonymous. "The South: Intruders in the Dust." *Time*, 23 Sept. 1966, pp. 26.

Anonymous. "When Integration Came After 12 Years." *US News and World Report*, 25 July 1966, p. 16.

Donelan, Richarde W., Gerald A. Neal, and Deneese L. Jones. "The Promise of Brown and the Reality of Academic Grouping: The Tracks of my Tears." *The Journal of Negro Education*, vol. 63, no. 3, 1994, pp. 376-87.

Evans-Winters, Venus E. "Are Black Girls Not Gifted? Race, Gender, and Resilience." *Interdisciplinary Journal of Teaching and Learning*, vol. 4, no. 1, 2014, pp. 22-30.

Federal Court. *Cunningham v. Grenada School District*, Federal Court Lawsuit, Civil Rights Movement Archive, www.crmvet.org/docs/66_grenada_school_suit.pdf. Accessed 2 July 2022.

Housee, Shirin, and Evonne Richards. "And Still We Rise: Stories of Resilience and Transgression." *Enhancing Learning in the Social Sciences*, vol. 3, no. 3, 2011, pp 1-22.

Karnes, Frances A., and Emily C. Collins. "State Definitions on the Gifted and Talented: A Report and Analysis." *Journal for the Education of the Gifted*, vol. 1, no 1, 1978, pp. 44-62.

Mildred J. Allen. Personal interview. 2001.

Montie, Mary. L. *Where Are All the Gifted Black Girls? Giving High School Girls Voice Via Qualitative Research Approach and Black Feminist Theory*. Dissertation. Wayne State University, 2013.

Owens, Marcia Allen. "Closet Chair and Committee Side Piece: Black Women STEM Faculty at HBCUs." *Presumed Incompetent II: Race, Class, Power, and Resistance of Women in Academia*, edited by Yolanda Flores Niemann et al., University Press of Colorado, 2020, pp. 233-44.

Owens, Marcia Allen. "Is That Healthy? Experiences of Microagressions by Black Women at Historically Black Institutions." *The Feminist Wire*, 2012, thefeministwire.com/2012/11/is-that-healthy-experiences-of-microaggressions-by-black-women-at-historically-black-institutions/. Accessed 2 July 2022.

Supreme Court of The United States. *U.S. Reports: Brown v. Board of Education*, 344 U.S. 1. 1952.

Upton, Rachel, and Courtney Tennenbaum. "The Role of Historically Black Colleges and Universities as Pathway Providers: Institutional Pathways to the STEM PhD among Black Students." *STEM at American Institutes for Research*. Sept. 2014.

Willie T. Allen. Personal interview, 1997.

Chapter 8

# Liminalities of the Mother

Jameka Hartley

## Betweenness

*Caterpillar: chrysalis :: aroused: drowsy*
*Baby: adolescent :: pregnancy: motherhood*
*Dusk: dawn :: purple: lavender*

When I took the Scholastic Aptitude Test commonly known as the SAT exam, almost two decades ago, I loved and hated analogy questions formatted like those above. I loved them because they were intriguing. I found great satisfaction in unlocking the riddle and getting the answer correct. I hated them because they were often written in a way that was deliberately obtuse. The key was in finding the relationship between the groups. It was this betweenness that I was drawn to.

> *Liminal (adj.): in-between, transitional*
> (Merriam-Webster)

I continue to be drawn to the in-betweenness of life—the phases of life that produce and (re)produce newer versions of self. A liminal space that I now find myself oscillating between is daughterhood and motherhood. I am a Black daughter raising two Black daughters. I am always both daughter and mother.

## Conceptualization of (Self) Identity

According to the communication theory of identity put forth by Michael L. Hecht et al., identity is located in four interconnected frames: personal, enacted, relational, and communal. The personal frame places identity at the locus within the self (i.e., self-image), whereas the enacted frame places it at the level of performative interaction with others (i.e., self-expression). The relational frame places identity within relationships themselves, such as friendships, romantic partners, and familial connections, whereas the communal frame places identity within the shared collective memory of a particular group of people. Each frame bleeds into the other and impacts and influences how identity is communicated both internally and externally.

Frames can have tensions between them where they may contradict or compete with one another. These tensions are referred to as identity gaps: "Identity gaps are defined as discrepancies between or among the four frames of identity.... One might posit that gaps always accompany communication and are present to some degree in all relationships" (Jung and Hecht 268). I extend their thinking to include one's relationship to/with the self. I think of these tensions less as gaps but as productive liminal spaces. My self-image has moved from daughter to daughtermother to daughter + mother. I have been my mother's daughter since I have had breath in my lungs. As an adult, I had the privilege of becoming a mother and my relational identity undulated between being both a daughter and a mother. I write daughtermother as one word because the dual identities of being my mother's daughter and a mother to my own children cannot be uncoupled. Each identity informs the other. My daughter-self was strengthened by the added relationship of mother. Through the communication exchanges I had with my own daughters, I constituted deeper understanding of my mother's love, adoration, devotion, and sacrifice for me.

A little over a month after my first Mother's Day, my mother died unexpectedly. I was a new mother who needed her mother to help her mother, and she was no longer physically present to mother me. Yet the embodied experience of mothering my daughter allowed me to keep myself afloat in an ocean of grief. Since my mother's transition starside, my daughter-self has been reconstituted again to daughter + mother. I write daughter + mother separately to honour my mother's transition. I will forever be her daughter as she will always be my mother even if she is not physically present in the same way as she once was. Using the "+" joins us the way that life and death as well as blood and bone continue to join us even now. Below, I offer autoethnographic vignettes and poems associated with each liminal state of my (self) identity.

## Liminal State One: Daughter

My mama was my first teacher
before I even knew what a teacher was.

School was in
all the time at our house.

Nintendo, Gameboy, Sega Genesis didn't have a place in my childhood.
Toys = educational opportunity
instead it was puzzles, books, Discovery Toys, and Gymboree.

My mama was such a good teacher, she taught me to teach myself...
unbeknownst to me
that's the beauty of a great educator
learning happens right under your nose.

Mama called it my activity bag. I had one wherever we went.
One for the car and one for travel.
It was full of age appropriate learnin'
readin' books, colorin' books, flashcards, galore.

If mommy had an adult meeting to attend and I was the only child there
I taught myself.
Me and my activity bag.

My mama taught me about life.
   About security/money/(agape) love/Black is beautiful/a woman's worth/the art of storytelling/mothering while Black/Jesus/church/
the difference
between the two/politics/lipsticks/and dicks.

—Mama Taught Me

\*\*\*

Growing up in a Black Baptist church, there were instances where our church congregation would visit another church for a special service, such as a pastor's anniversary or women's day program. This special service was usually in the afternoon or evening, in addition to the regular church services that either congregation hosted that day. As the visiting church, your pastor would offer the sermon, bring his own choir, and church members were encouraged to attend to support their home pastor while travelling for his speaking engagement. It is common at these joint services for a welcome to be offered to the guest church and for a member of the guest congregation to offer a response.

We had travelled on the church bus to get to Seventh Street Baptist Church so Reverend Murray could offer forth the Word. I was sitting next to my mom, people watching, noticing how different their sanctuary was to ours. A deacon stood at the lectern and said, "We'd like to welcome Reverend Murray and the members of First Baptist Church for joining us on this joyous occasion of Pastor Clayman's thirtieth anniversary of Seventh Street. To God be the glory for the great things He has done. We'll now have a response from First Baptist."

Deacon Porter from our church rose and said, "Little Debby will you come and offer our response? Little Debby?"

I looked around waiting to see which member of our church would respond to his question when I felt my mom nudging me. I gave her a questioning look.

"Little Debby?" I heard again.

"He means you. Go on up there." My mother, Debby, instructed. I obliged.

\*\*\*

Little Debbie is a snack cake, but I am more than that.

I AM little Debby.

With my quick wit and sharp tongue
"Oh, you speak so well" they say
For what?
       A kid?
              A Black kid?
                     A Black girl?

Yes. I do speak well because
I AM little Debby.

This apple doesn't fall far from the tree.
Apples are sweet. Not as sweet as snack cakes but sweet in their own right.

Mommy loves Granny Smith. I'm partial to Honeycrisp.
The red to her green and everything in between

I AM little Debby

—Little Debby


That is what it was like as my mother's daughter. I was seen by others as an extension of her while simultaneously being my self. DebbyandJameka. JamekaandDebby.

> *Liminal (adj.): of, relating to, or being an intermediate state, phase, or condition*
> (Merriam-Webster)

It is holy ground
To sit between the thighs that birthed you.

For plaits or twists or puffs
For parts oiled
For healing naps and scalps.

Caring for young long after the womb
Fourth trimester or fortieth.
Forty acres and a mule
They promised us.

Black mothers suckled babies in the hull of cargo ships.
We nursed babies we didn't bear
Still
Today
We are birthing this nation anew
Demanding our due.

Melanated maternal mortality rates are climbing.
Our babies are dying
Yet we are not new to this
We are true to this.

The sacrament of blood and cervical fluid
Pays homage to the wombs before us
And testimony to the strength within.

This motherhood.
This womanhood.
This Black.
It... is... all...

revolutionary.

—Between

## Liminal State Two: Daughtermother

Who am I?

I am my mother's daughter.
It is us.

Her and I.
    I and she.
        We.

Sometimes it feels like we're being boiled like corn n' potatoes in this pot called life.
The past at our backs
The world our oyster or maybe more like our crawfish.
Pinch/Twist/Suck/Savor.

Still you ask
Who am I?

I am my mother's love
made flesh.
Papa's sometimes
but Mama's baby
all ways
always.

***

I became a mom before I had a baby to hold in my arms and nurse at my breasts. I endured three miscarriages before my first daughter made her way Earthside. My mother's influence and imprint are reflected in every area of my life but particularly in how I mother. Becoming a mother gave me a true appreciation for our connection as mother and daughter and the choices she had made in mothering me. Breastfeeding into toddlerhood, baby wearing, cloth diapering, and making homemade baby food all became a part of my mother-self and were borne directly from my mother's maternal legacy.

There used to be bracelets that people of the Christian faith sported proudly that said "WWJD...What Would Jesus Do?" My mother-self asks daily "WWMD... What Would Mommy Do? What did Mommy Do?" Each age and stage of childhood present me with a fresh set of memory mapping to complete and follow accordingly while mothering my daughters.

***

My mother was a logophile, a lover of words. As a child she would read the dictionary for fun and immerse herself in a world of words. She had an eloquent command of language and would write beautiful letters. The only thing I wanted on my first Mother's Day was a written letter of my mother's impressions of my mother-self. What mother had I communicated to her? She gave me that letter, and it is one of my most treasured possessions. I learned to love words through her. and I aspire to instill that same love of words into my daughters. One of the ways I started to extend the logophile legacy was that I began to write to my oldest daughter shortly after she was born. Below is one of those entries.

*My dearest daughter,*

*I've seen a few quotes lately that made me think of us and our relationship: "I can't settle for just anything. My daughter is watching me" and "We have to be the examples we want our daughters to be." I reflect a lot on choices I made before you arrived and of the things I want to shield you from having to experience. I tell you things that will build you up because words have power. You are the manifestation of words, of prayers. I prayed about your sweet spirit (among other things) and God listened. I'm excited about your future. I'm curious as to what your first word will be. It warms my heart when you hug me or blow me kisses or give me kisses. It's the absolute best. The joy you bring is unmatched. I love being your mama.*

*I had a conversation with your dad today, and we were discussing how having kids impacts your marriage. Your dad mentioned a school of thought that parents can lose themselves in their children. I think I've found myself since having you and becoming your mom. Being your mom makes me clearer about what type of woman I am and what type of woman I want to be. I know how much my mom influenced me in a positive way, and I want to be that light and role model for you as well.*

*Love,*
*Mommy*

***

*Liminal (adj.): of, relating to, or situated at a sensory threshold*
(Merriam-Webster)

## Liminal State Three: Daughter + Mother

*My dearest daughter,*

*Your Mimi died today, July 31, 2017. My mother. Your grandmother. She was and is the best woman I know. The mom I am to you is because of her. I look forward to sharing lots of pictures and stories with you about her. She was/is incredible. She loved you so very much, and seeing you made her so happy. She'll be your guardian angel. I'm sorry that you won't have more time with her here on Earth, but you'll get lots of time with her in eternity. Up until now, I haven't put dates in this journaling project, but I want you to know this one. It's important.*

*I pray that you and I will have the type of relationship I had with her. One of love, respect, admiration, fun, laughter, friendship. Your Mimi was one of my closest/best friends as well as my mom. We had the mother-daughter friendship that grows and deepens in adulthood. I could tell your Mimi anything, even though I didn't act on that all the time but the same goes for you. You can tell me anything, and I do hope you'll act on it. I love you. Your Mimi would want you to keep on keepin' on (that was one of her sayings).*

*Love,*
*Mommy*

***

Grief was the sensory threshold I found myself at in 2017. My daughter-self and mother-self were competing to reconcile this new reality. When you are grieving, people can say hurtful things unintentionally. One of the phrases that has been said to me on many occasions is that I no longer have a mother. This statement is untrue. I have a mother. She is not here with me physically, but her absence on Earth does not render her mother-self obsolete.

During my first pregnancy and birthing experience, my spouse was on a military deployment. My mother filled in as my birth partner and support. We attended birthing classes together, put together baby furniture, and cooked together to stock up the freezer with meals. My mother witnessed her daughter cross the threshold from daughter to daughtermother. My oldest daughter came into this world the same way I did—through a crescent moon warrior cut also known as a C-section. My mother bore witness and stood in the liminal space of my selves as she watched the obstetrician lift my daughter from my womb.

When I got pregnant again, it was bittersweet. I was pleased about the new life that was growing in my womb and simultaneously saddened that I would have an entire pregnancy and birth experience without my mother. Fortunately, I had resolved the conflict of my daughter-self and mother-self by then. I knew myself to be both daughter + mother.

## Conclusion

*Liminal (adj.): of, related to a blurring of what was, what is, and what is to come: a becoming*

(Jameka Hartley, author)

```
    e and f
s           a
 i           l
r            l
```

Our chests in unison. Our breath, one.
Your toasted brown skin is the same as mine.
You are an extension of me yet still you.
May we always remember our breath
in tandem.

—breastfeeding/breastfed/legacy

The borders of my identity continue to bleed. Motherhood has shown me this more than any other identity I currently inhabit. Motherhood exists outside of the relational frame and into the communal frame. "Mother" is absolutely a false boundary that can limit social possibility, as Bryant K. Alexander argues. What a mother is and who a mother is are all contested identities, yet each mother knows herself as daughter and mother within each frame: personal, enacted, relational, and communal.

Despite the porous frames that constitute identity, mothers are treated as finite and definitive. This conceptualization is reductionist. Mothers are constantly in progress. Each mother is learning as they go while adapting to the wild unknown that is parenting. We are being born again and again alongside our children. We are a multiplicity of liminalities.

## Works Cited

Alexander, Bryant K. "Critical Autoethnography as Intersectional Praxis: A Performative Pedagogical Interplay on Bleeding Borders of Identity." *Critical Autoethnography: Intersecting Cultural Identities in Everyday Life*, edited by Robin Boylorn and Mark Orbe, Routledge, 2014, pp. 110-122.

Hecht, Michael L., et al. "A Communication Theory of Identity: Development, Theoretical Perspective, and Future Directions." *Theorizing about Intercultural Communication*, edited by William B. Gudykunst, Sage, 2005, pp. 257-78.

Jung, Eura, and Michael L. Hecht. "Elaborating the Communication Theory of Identity: Identity Gaps and Communication Outcomes." *Communication Quarterly*, vol. 52, no. 3, 2004, pp. 265-83.

"Liminal." *Merriam-Webster*, www.merriam-webster.com/dictionary/liminal. Accessed 2 July 2022.

Chapter 9

# Nitaawigiwin: A Ceremony of Thinking about My Anishinaabeg Mother

Renee E. Mazinegiizhigoo-kwe Bedard

At each stage of my two daughters' lives, I thought about my late mother Shirley Ida Bédard. In this chapter, I discuss the Anishinaabeg ceremony of nitaawigiwin (cord, placenta, and amniotic sac collection and burial), which is meant to invoke the maternal chain of relationships linking my late mother, ancestral grandmothers, my daughters, and myself. Through the nitaawigiwin ceremony, I revitalized and renewed our family's lost maternal traditions and ancestral connections. Overall, this chapter aims to explore nitaawigiwin as a site of resurgence of maternal cultural traditions, gender norms, and philosophies of living.

As I performed Anishinaabeg maternal rites of birth and postnatal traditions, I felt the absence of my mother deeply but also a renewed sense of her presence both spiritually and emotionally. I learned that this was due to revitalization of the madjimadzuin (maternal lifeline) traditions embedded in the ceremony of nitaawigiwin, which reawakens the ancestral links, especially those damaged by the impact of colonization. Through the nitaawigiwin ceremonial traditions and teachings, I thought about and felt reconnected to my late Anishinaabeg mother. In this chapter, I will explore the teachings of majimadzuin, which inform the philosophical and ontological knowledge of the ceremony of nitaawigiwin. Next, I will examine the teachings and cultural customs practiced within the nitaawigiwin ceremony, particularly, through the lens of my own experiences. To conclude, I will explore my thoughts as well as my own mothering journey through the ceremony of nitaawigiwin from the lens of an Anishinaabeg maternal perspective.

## Madjimadzuin

With my first pregnancy, I was introduced to the concept of madjimadzuin through the teachings of my Indigenous midwives. Madjimadzuin is a teaching showing how we are all related, even to those who are no longer living and those yet to be born. It is the spiritual link anchoring us to our ancestors, which reaches back through time to the creation of the first human beings—the first women and mothers, who walked gently upon Mother-the-Earth. Madjimadzuin teachings reveal the intergenerational connections and maternal links between great-grandmothers, grandmothers, mothers, daughters, and granddaughters in a constant spiral through time, space, and spirit. According to Anishinaabeg linguist James Vukelich, "I am all of my relatives and all of my relatives are me" (Ojibwe Word of the Day Gidinawendimin). He explains that our relationships as human beings span time, space, and multiple realities, for example, the Land of the Spirits. We are inextricably connected to one another through our blood and our jichaag (soul-spirit), which is contained with the physical and metaphysical nature of the madjimadzuin.

Madjimadzuin contains four physical components. First is the placenta, which is called the binoojiizhensim odapikweshimon (Ningewance 97) in Anishinaabemowin (the Anishinaabeg language). The placenta is called the "life-carrier" or "life-protector," and for this reason it is shaped like a shield (Anderson 50). According to Métis/Cree scholar Kim Anderson, the placenta is described as sacred because it holds a "life-force" that the mother shares with her child, and the placenta carries this to the baby (50). Next is the umbilical cord, which delivers nutrients to the baby from the mother. This cord is called the odiseyaab (Ningewance 128). Anderson notes that umbilical cords "signified connections that were made between the child and his or her relations" (51). Third is the amniotic sac, which encompasses the baby inside the womb of the mother. This is referred to as gaa-izhibiindenig abinoojiizhens onibiim jibwaa-nitaawigid (Ningewance 17). Last are the amniotic waters, which hold several traditional names. First, it is known as mide-waaboo, which means the sacred "water of life" or the "sacred water essential for growing life" (Best Start Resource Centre 26). Second, it is referred to as abinoojiizhens onibiim (Ningewance 17) or abinoojii onibiim. Abinoojiizhens means a very small baby who is not yet born. Onibiim means "s/he has water," or "she holds water." Although these four components—the umbilical cord, placenta, amniotic sac, and amniotic water—are the physical representation of madjimadzuin, the connection is also a spiritual lifeline that is multi-dimensional, which spans time and space and binds the spirit world to the everyday world we live in.

In 1929, anthropologist Diamond Jenness documented the Anishinaabeg concept of the metaphysical components of madjimadzuin. Jenness listened to the stories and teachings that the Anishinaabeg of Wasauksing First Nation (Parry Island) shared about fertility, conception, and birth of new life. The Anishinaabek of Wasauksing taught Jenness about the concept of "madjimadzuin," which means the "moving life-line" or "moving life." Madjimadzuin reveals that Anishinaabeg women play a central role as the metaphysical and physical vessels for conception, the first doorway of life, those who nourish the children of the nation, and the first teachers our people have in what it means to be Anishinaabeg. Jenness notes that women were the guardians and protectors responsible for maintaining the chain of "moving life" (90).

The teachings on the madjimadzuin are embedded in the stories and teachings of Jiibay-Miikana (Milky Way; the Path of Souls; the Spirit Trail). Wasauksing community members shared with Jenness the following about Jiibay-Miikana:

> [It] is an enormous bucket-handle that holds the earth in place; if it ever breaks the world will come to an end. The "life-line" is a human Milky Way; it is the chain of ancestors connecting those who have gone before with those who follow, the line of ancestors and descendants together with all the inheritance factors they carry with them. (Jenness 90)

In the stories, the Jiibay-Miikana is the pathway for souls to travel from this earthly realm to the Spirit realm (Johnston, *Ojibway Ceremonies* 150). As the vessels of conception, women are the doorways for new spirits to enter this realm and therefore are guardians responsible for maintaining this chain of "moving life" (Jenness 90). The Anishinaabeg have many teachings on the qualities of the umbilical cord as the embodiment of the "human life-line." Jenness refers to Anishinaabeg and Omàmiwininiwak (Algonquin) beliefs of the umbilical cord as a version of a "human milky way." He explains that the umbilical cord acts like a "chain connecting those who have gone before with those who follow the line of ancestors and descendants together with all of the inheritance factors they carry with them" (90).

Anishinaabeg women are taught that they must protect the madjimadzuin after birth and to collect the parts of its physical form. Anishinaabeg mothers play a critical role in maintaining the continuity of the lifeline and chain of ancestors, for as Basil Johnston writes on the holistic understanding of mino-bimaadiziwin (that is, life lived in a good way): "There is continuity, there is no break" (*Ojibway Heritage* 117). The Anishinaabeg call the collection of the madjimadzuin following birth the nitaawigiwin ceremony, which is performed by mothers by collecting the parts of the physical representation of the madjimadzuin: the placenta, the cord, and the amniotic sac. These three components are then gifted to the land so that the child forms their madjimadzuin with Aki, the land.

## Nitaawigiwin: A Ceremony of Thinking about My Anishinaabeg Mother

Among the Anishinaabeg, a mother's role is to introduce our children to mino-bimaadiziwin. Minogi'aawasowin is what we call the traditional way that Anishinaabeg mothers engage with the good way of childrearing. The purpose being to develop a child's mind, body, spirit, and emotional wellbeing. We foster minogi'aawasowin through our maternal ceremonies and knowledge systems, which at puberty and pregnancy are shared with us by our mothers, grandmothers, and the mindimooyenyag (old wise women; women Elders) of our communities. Minogi'aawaso translates to the act of raising children in a good way, and minogi'aawasowin refers to the ways we engage in the process of raising children to be good Anishinaabeg, both human beings and good citizens of the nation. The process of rearing begins at birth and in the postnatal period just after birth, when a mother begins her ceremony of nitaawigiwin.

Nitaawigi translates to "s/he is born; s/he grows, grows up." A child undergoes a ceremonial rite of passage from birth out of the Spirit World and into life on this earthly world. The umbilical cord, placenta, and amniotic sac connect the child to the Spirit World. They are physical reminders of that realm of existence. That connection is physically severed from the mother as the doorway when the placenta and amniotic sac are delivered and the umbilical cord is cut. The spiritual cord within the madjimadzuin is then transferred through the nitaawigiwin ceremony to the land; however, a portion always remains connecting mother to baby, which is why mothers collect and keep the stump of the cord in a small leather pouch.

Nitaawigiwin is the beginning of the process of rearing a child into knowing what it means to be a human being: an Anishinaabe-kwe (female; woman), Anishinaabeg-nini (male; man), or Anishinaabe-niizh-manidoowag (Two-Spirited, male/female, LGBTQIQQ2SA+, or queer/trans). The mother collects the physical parts of the madjimadzuin to begin the process of rearing her child in the Anishinaabeg way of being, living, doing, seeing, and relating to the cosmos. In this way, the nitaawigiwin ceremony ushers an Anishinaabeg child onto the path of mino-bimaadiziwin.

## Collection of the Madjimadzuin (Cord, Placenta, and Amniotic Sac)

The first part of the nitaawigiwin is something I thought long about and wished I could have had my mother's presence while I underwent a birth that did not go as planned. Once the amniotic fluid as well as the cord, placenta, and amniotic sac are birthed, the mother initiates the nitaawigiwin ceremony. The amniotic fluid signals that the nitaawigiwin will begin because it cleanses the way for new life to enter from the Spirit Realm. Both my daughters were born in southern Ontario, Canada, so we collected and stored these items in our freezer until we could make the trek back up to northern Ontario to bury their madjimadzuin together. For me, I needed to collect, hold on to, and carry the madjimadzuin of my daughters back home to ensure their cultural identity and their connection to the territory of their grandmothers.

## Collection of the Odisiins (Fallen Navel Stump)

As part of the madjimadzuin, the odisiins (navel stump) is considered sacred. The odis (navel or belly button) is our physical reminder of the intimate connection we have with our mothers, both biological and spiritual. Once the first collection occurs, a mother waits for the odisiins to dry up naturally and fall off the baby to reveal the odis. Anishinaabeg mothers place the stump with semaa (tobacco) into a small leather hide pouch. She may choose to keep it in her possession forever or place it in nature at a time of her choosing. Some women choose to bury it. In accordance with this tradition, Anishinaabeg scholars Thomas Peacock and Marlene Wisuri write:

> The navel cord represents the lifelong connection of mother and baby. In some ancient communities, the mother and baby would take the navel-cord bag into the woods and bury it at the end of the first year of the baby's life. This signified that it was time for the baby to develop as an individual and to someday go off on its own, apart from its mother. In other communities, the mother kept the navel cord and gave it to the child when he or she got older. (37)

Additionally, a navel cord pouch could be buried under specific medicine plants important to a woman's fertility, health, and wellbeing, and for boys the navel cord pouch could be dropped in the place of their first hunt and kill (51).

Other women hang the pouch inside on a tree branch, thus ensuring that the individual has a good sense of their territorial lands and can become a good hunter, fisherman or woman, or gatherer of plant food and medicines. In her book *Life Stages and Native Women: Memory, Teachings, and Story Medicine*, Anderson shares the teachings of Anishinaabekwe Marie Anderson, who teaches that Anishinaabeg women put their babies' umbilical cords into a bag and tie them up in a tree or dig a hole at the root of the tree and bury the cord under the root (51-52). She explains that the purpose "establishes a connection between the lifelong journey of the child, the young and old of the community, and the land" (51-52).

I was taught that our women would hang the pouch on the rounded headframe of the dikinaagan (cradle board; baby board; bowl of the earth), which is a traditional baby carrier used by Kwewag to transport their babies on their backs. The pouches are believed to offer protection from spiritual attacks that might take the baby's spirit back to the Land of Spirits. The pouch was used—along with a bawaajige-nagwaaganan (dreamcatcher) made of miskwaabiimizh (red willow)—to not only protect the child's spirit but also to promote the overall healthy development of proper eyesight and mental acuity. Furthermore, there is the belief that the pouch would lead to a calm baby rather than a baby that was often fussy and easily agitated; fussy babies are believed to be looking for their odisiiyaab (cord). If not hung from the dikinaagan, the pouch was hung around the baby's neck, shielding the hollow of the neck, which is considered vital to a human being's life-force energies.

Anishinaabeg Elders Lee Staples and Chato Gonzalez offer some teachings on the collection of the Odisiins, stating: "At the time of birth a baby has a small scab on his bellybutton. Once that scab falls off of his bellybutton, the scab is kept. It is put into a little bag with tobacco. That is what Anishinaabe called odisiins. Anishinaabe have always held on to that bellybutton. At the time of death, Anishinaabe took his bellybutton with him." In another teaching, Anishinaabeg Elders Lee Staples and Melissa Boyd say that mothers keep the odisiins and care for it so that our children always feel like a whole person in body, mind, and spirit. To ensure that our children grow up feeling complete inside, Anishinaabeg Elder Lee Staples advises that "When Anishinaabe has lost something and is forever looking around for it, he is jokingly asked, 'What are you looking for? Are you looking for your bellybutton?'" (Staples and Gonzalez). Regarding the odisiinsag of my own daughters, I followed protocols and ethics as a way to nurture a healthy sense of identity as kwezens in body, mind, and spirit.

I carry my daughters' odisiinsag in a hide pouch, inside my medicine bundle, which holds items I consider sacred for ceremony, traditional medicines, and keepsake items connected to my identity. When I look at the hide pouch holding the odisiinsag of my daughters, I recall waiting and waiting for the stumps to fall off. I remember with my first daughter the feelings of being both grossed out by the odisiinsag and loving it. But I was also sad when it fell off because it was the last physical reminder of the connection I had to her from her time in the womb. As mothers, we mourn our pregnancies; to keep that little stump is a lasting reminder of that precious time.

I have baby keepsakes from my mother that I cherish because she cherished them. Maternal keepsakes are a mother's right and evidence of a deep and abiding relationship that spans time and space. For me, the odisiins is a sign of the treaty I have with my child. I carried my children in my womb, and I breastfed each girl for over a year, sharing my body as nourishment and comfort. We taught each other how to balance giving, taking, and sharing. Together, we learned that "One nation cannot dominate over the other. One nation cannot control all of the land and all of the resources" (Simpson 107). When my ancestors entered into treaties with other nations, gifts and keepsakes of those events were taken, preserved, and cherished as symbols of those relationships. Michi Saagiig Nishnaabeg scholar Leanne Betasamosake Simpson explains that "treaties are ultimately about a relationship." Simpson continues: "The relationship comes first above all else, above the pain. It is about commitment and compassion. It is about a love of the land and a love for the people" (107-08). The odisiins is symbolic reminder for not only the treaty relationships I hold with my children but also those I still maintain with my mother, whom I am still connected to, along with those grandmothers seven generations back and those grandchildren seven generations yet to come. I will carry my children's odisiinag all my life or until I go back to the territory of my ancestors to live in the branches of a nookomis-giizhik (cedar tree) on the shores of the French River, but I will let my heart guide me with regarding that decision.

## Choosing the Site for Burial

The nitaawigiwin ceremony concludes with the burial of the cord, placenta, and amniotic sac. The mother will search for a place to establish her child's madjimadzuin with the land. The role of the mother is to go out on the land of their own mother and grandmothers and look for a spot to bury the madjimadzuin. They will look for a nookomis-giizhisag (grandmother cedar), zhingobiig (sister balsam), or a patch of ode'iminan (heart berries or wild strawberries), which all hold significant meanings to women's fertility. This is where the mother will bury the madjimadzuin belonging to her child so that it will become one with the land. This is an important decision because the child's jichaag (soul spirit) and madjimadzuin will be connected to that spot on the earth for the rest of their life. Once she finds the right place, she lays her semaa (sacred tobacco) down. Next, prayers are offered to Gizhew-Manidoo and Aki. Then she will introduce herself to the tree and state her intentions. When talking to a living being from the plant world, mashkikiiwikwe (medicine woman) Mary Siisip Geniusz advises that we need to "really talk to the plant" and reassure it that you mean no harm to it or to its "grandchildren [who] will live after you" (23). The mother will ask the tree if it is okay to leave her child's madjimadzuin with the tree so that it might form a connection to the land and territory of their grandmothers. Anishinaabeg believe that permission is paramount when asking anything of another living being. Waiting for a sign, such as a branch blowing on the breeze, a leaf falling or a rustling of leaves, she will then know it is okay to proceed to put the baby's madjimadzuin in the earth below the ojiibikan (roots) of the tree.

When the mother comes to the tree or plant requesting to perform her burial rites, but no sign of permission is given, then the answer is a firm "no." When this rejection happens, it is best for the mother to find another location. We must always respect the rights of other living beings to say "no." Consent is a vital ethical consideration and integral to upholding the gichi-inaakonigewin (Great laws of Creation; laws of Gizhew-Manidoo; laws of nature).

When I performed this part of the ceremony, my husband found a basa'igaan (grove of cedars) as the place we would call for the help of the plant world to take the madjimadzuin of our children and connect them to their traditional territory. Cedar trees are significant because of the sacredness they have to all Anishinaabeg but especially to women. Geniusz writes as follows: "Grandmother Cedar has within her very growth the balance of Creation, and she ties the four levels of our physical world to the four levels of the Spirit world. Calling for help with cedar is available to Anishinaabeg" (37). In fact, at the end of this ceremony, mothers can take some of the cedar back home and hang it near where their child sleeps or on the arched frame of the dikinaagan (Geniusz 41). The cedar continues to protect the child with grandmotherly love. I carry some cedar in my bundle from the location where my daughters' madjimadzuin are buried.

At the location, each of my family members was given tobacco to lay on the earth to ask permission to dig a hole and lay the madjimadzuin down below the roots of the tree we chose. I asked Nookomis-Giizik to welcome my children as Anishinaabe-kwezens and her granddaughters. I introduced us, and then we prayed and waited for permission. We stayed quiet, watched, and listened for direction from the basa'igaan. We felt drawn to one location and one area near the tree, and taking that as the sign we needed, we set about digging a deep hole among the ojiibikan (roots).

Once the hole was about one-and-a-half to two feet down, we stopped to unwrap the two madjimadzuin and placed them together. Next, we found and placed heavy granite stones on them so that animals could not dig them out. My husband and daughters then finished burying the madjimadzuin, and we concluded by speaking to the girls about the importance of the ceremony. They wanted to place special items on top of the spot to adorn it, so they placed flowers, colourful leaves, and stones they felt were special. We told them they were now connected to Aki, the earth, through their buried madjimadzuin as well as to their mommy and Kokum (grandmother) Shirley as well as Gchi-Kokum Roseanne Dokis (great-grandmother). To conclude the ceremony, everyone said our thank you to Aki and Nookomis-Giizhik, and we left feeling like we had accomplished something important for our family. My overall goal was to foster both of my daughters' path of mino-bimaadiziwin, or living that good life as human beings as well as their path of kwezens (little girls), which would give my children the cultural heritage and knowledge of their ancestors. Nitaawigiwin is my legacy to my daughters and future granddaughters.

## Concluding Thoughts

My mother told a story that our ancestors used to hide their valuables from the priests so that they would not be confiscated by the church. They would put ceremonial items, silver, and money in metal boxes or birchbark containers that they buried among the roots of trees. At the time of her telling me this story, neither one of us knew about the nitaawigiwin ceremony, but when I learned about it, I thought of her story and about her. I have come full circle with the ways of my ancestors. I buried my valuables among the roots of the trees not out of fear of loss but out a desire for cultural revitalization and resurgence.

To honour my mother and ancestral grandmothers, I want to finish with a poem I wrote to summarize this chapter, Miigwech! Thank you!

## Roots

Dear daughters, together in time, like links in a chain.
I buried your madjimadzuin deep under the roots of Nookomis-Giizhik.
There you will be safe. There you will be protected. There I will think of you.

Dear daughters, together we will take root,
as a family, together and apart, like links in a chain.

Dear mother, I gathered the ways of my grandmothers before me,
and together we will become Anishinaabe-kwewag again,
connected forever like links in a chain.

Dear mother, I buried the precious things below Nookomis-Giizhik,
among the roots and earth so dark, it reminded me of our hair.
They won't take our precious things anymore mother.

Dear daughters and dear mother, together we take root,
as a family, like links in a chain.

*I think of you*, my daughters.
*I think of you*, my mother.
Like links in a chain.
Madjimadzuin!
Madjimadzuin!
Madjimadzuin!

## Endnotes

1. "Anishinaabeg" is an umbrella term for those nations rooted in the same linguistic dialect, cultural teachings, and intellectual traditions. Those who use the term to describe themselves as Anishinaabe (meaning human being) are composed of the following nations: Anishiniwag (Oji-Cree), Ojibweg, Odaawaag, Bodéwadmik, Odishkwaamagiig (Nipissing), Misizaagiwininiwag (Mississaugas), Omàmiwininiwak (Algonquin), and Leni Lenape (Delaware). The Anishinaabeg inhabit the Great Lakes region in both Canada and the United States. In Anishinaabemowin (Anishinaabeg language), the word "Anishinaabeg" means the original human beings (Benton-Banai).

## Works Cited

"Abinoojii onibiim." *Translate Ojibwe*, www.translateojibwe.com/en/dictionary-ojibwe-english/onibiim. Accessed 12 July 2022.

"Abinoojiizhens+ag." *Translate Ojibwe*, www.translateojibwe.com/en/dictionary-english-ojibwe/baby. Accessed 12 July 2022.

Anderson, Kim. *Life Stages and Native Women: Memory, Teachings, and Story Medicine*. University of Manitoba Press, 2011.

"Anishinaabe." *The Ojibway People's Dictionary*, ojibwe.lib.umn.edu/main-entry/anishinaabe-na Accessed 12 July 2022.

Best Start Resource Centre. *Beginning Journey: First Nations Pregnancy Resource*. Best Start Resource Centre, 2013.

Benton-Banai, Edward. *The Mishomis Book: The Voice of the Ojibway*. University of Minnesota Press, 1988.

"Binoojiinhyag gaa-abidjig." *Translate Ojibwe*, www.translateojibwe.com/en/dictionary-ojibwe-english/abinoojiinhyag+gaa-abidjig. Accessed 12 July 2022.

Geniusz, Mary Siisip. *Plants Have So Much to Give Us, All We Have to Do is Ask: Anishinaabe Botanical Teachings*. University of Minnesota Press, 2015.

Jenness, Diamond. *The Ojibwa Indians of Parry Island, Their Social and Religious Life*. National Museum of Canada, 1935.

Johnston, Basil. *Ojibway Ceremonies*. McClelland Stewart, 1982.

Johnston, Basil. *Ojibway Heritage*. McClelland and Stewart, 2008.

"Minogi'aawaso," *The Ojibwe People's Dictionary*, ojibwe.lib.umn.edu/main-entry/minogi-aawaso-vai. Accessed 12 July 2022.

Ningewance, Agnes, et al. *Ojibwe Medical Dictionary A Handbook for Health Care Providers*. www.slmhc.on.ca/assets/files/traditional-healing/medical_dictionary_ojibwe.pdf. Accessed 12 July 2022.

"Nitaawigi." *The Ojibwe People's Dictionary*, ojibwe.lib.umn.edu/main-entry/nitaawigi-vai. Accessed 12 July 2022.

"Onibiim." *The Ojibwe People's Dictionary*, ojibwe.lib.umn.edu/main-entry/onibiimi-vai. Accessed 12 July 2022.

"Ozhigi." *The Ojibwe People's Dictionary*, ojibwe.lib.umn.edu/main-entry/ozhigi-vai. Accessed 12 July 2022.

Peacock, Thomas, and Marlene Wisuri. *The Four Hills of Life: Ojibwe Wisdom*. Minnesota Historical Society Press, 2006.

Simpson, Leanne. *Dancing on Our Turtle's Back: Stories of Nishnaabeg Re-Creation, Resurgence and a New Emergence*. ARP Books, 2011.

Staples, Lee, and Chato Gonzalez. "Odisiins A Child's Bellybutton." *Ojibwe Inaajimowin: The Story as It's Told*, vol. 18, no. 7, July 2016m www.millelacsband.com/content/8-news/inaajimowin-archive/1607-inaajimovin.pdf. Accessed 12 July 2022.

Staples, Lee, and Melissa Boyd. "Waakobinigod A'aw Anishinabe—That Which Pulls Anishinaabe From the Original Teachings." *Ojibwe Inaajimowin: The Story as It's Told*, vol. 20, no. 3, March 2018. Accessed 12 July 2022.

Vukelich, James. "Ojibwe Word of the Day Gidinawendimin. ᑭᓇᐌᐣᑎᒥᐧ 'We Are Related to Each Other.'" *Facebook*, 23 July 2020, www.facebook.com/james.vukelich.7/videos/989476848486846/. Accessed 12 July 2022.

Weechi it te win Family Services and the Fort Francis Governance Team. *Childcare Practices: Raising Our Children the Anishinaabe Way*. www.weechi.ca/. Accessed 12 July 2022.

# Part III

Ritual, Art, and Literature

Chapter 10

# Perspectives on Motherhood through the Lens of Postmemory and Artistic Practice

Sylvia Griffin

The mother-daughter relationship has long been acknowledged as one of primary importance and central to the development of healthy attachments throughout one's life. In this chapter, I relate how being parented by a traumatized mother affected my childhood, my expectations, and own experiences of motherhood. I do this through the lens of postmemory (or intergenerational) trauma theory, as defined by the academic Marianne Hirsch. I address how this form of trauma can be unwittingly transmitted to subsequent generations, as illustrated by my relationship with my daughter and grandchildren. I then discuss how art can offer a safe means to navigate unsettling topics and relate how I have used my art practice to work through my experiences, referring to two projects by way of demonstration.

## Some Background

My family, Hungarian Jews who survived the atrocities of World War II, migrated to Australia in the late 1950s. I was born soon after their arrival. Living in the depths of suburban Sydney immediately set them apart, and the assumed superiority and casual racism of our neighbourhood served to "other" them—something that I intuited even at a young age. Within our family, a complex dynamic of selective reminiscences emerged, where fond memories of a past home resided alongside a painful family history. While we children knew that the Holocaust had affected the lives of our parents' immediate and extended family and acquaintances, it was not a topic that was easily approached or navigated.

My mother spent the latter part of her adolescence in German-occupied Budapest. My questions regarding this history were often deflected, met with silence, or worst of all with anguish. Although these responses were undoubtedly symptomatic of my family's unresolved trauma and bereavement, it served to colour my own worldview in a particular way: Feelings of anxiety and vulnerability accompanied my childhood as did a sense of guilt and responsibility for what I perceived to be my parents' burden of sadness. Writing on the effect of unspoken trauma on childhood development, academic Gita Arjan refers to this as nonverbal communication: "Within the silent emptiness, children acquired a helpless, automatic identification with parental feelings and their burden of intense despondency" (121).

I discovered that this sadness—bound closely to past traumatic events—often typified the generation who had lived through the Holocaust. Of even greater interest to me was the phenomenon of postmemory or inherited memory—that is, the unwitting passing down of trauma, anxiety, and sadness to subsequent generations to be absorbed and integrated into their beings. I also recognized that absence was a defining concept that could manifest in several ways. The death or unknown fate of loved ones hung over the living; objects often stood in for the absent person or could act as triggers to the past, and the passing of time often served to emphasize loss. It became clear to me that my parents—like most of their fellow survivors—had not only denied themselves the opportunity to properly grieve but had been actively discouraged to do so; the post-war emphasis seemed to be on getting on with the future. The stoicism that my parents and relatives adopted often translated as a disregard for any hardships that my siblings and I encountered, leaving us to feel unsupported and that our difficulties paled beside what they had experienced. In my mother's case, this also manifested as emotional distancing and an inability to cope with stressful situations.

## Postmemory: Mothers and Daughters

In the 1990s, academic Marianne Hirsch coined the term "postmemory" to describe the relationship that the next generation bears to the personal, collective, and cultural trauma of those before them—experiences they intuit and remember only by means of the stories, images, and behaviours that they grew up with. These experiences are often so deeply and affectively transmitted to them as to appear to constitute memories in their own right (Hirsch, "Surviving Images"). The power of this form of memory is when, to quote Hirsch, "its connection to its object or source is mediated not through recollection but through speech, on the invisible rather than the visible, and a highly selective point of view" (Hirsch, "The Generation of Postmemory" 9). Prior to this, researchers had considered intergenerational trauma alongside complex posttraumatic stress disorder (CPTSD) as a term to describe how the effects of a traumatic event could be passed down from one generation to the next (Caruth). Whereas earlier research mainly concentrated on Holocaust survivors, Hirsch applied postmemory more broadly and focused on the ongoing effects of past events in the present and alternative ways in which trauma could be communicated, shared, and worked through, including such mediums as art and literature.

Hirsch refers to the consequences of postmemory trauma on the mother-daughter dynamic and distinguishes between the different forms of traumatic memory and trauma transmission between survivor mothers and their daughters. The first is overidentification, in which the daughter appropriates the mother's memories, and the second is when silences or lack of communication can rupture the relationship and/or create an atmosphere where the daughter is left to fill in the gaps. Both forms of transmission invariably involve a degree of overlap and as Hirsch notes, although the various modes are neither mutually exclusive nor oppositional, postmemory is also subject to "different, if always overlapping, modes of 'remembering'" (Hirsch, "The Generation of Postmemory" 82).

My relationship with my mother falls into the second category of trauma transmission. Although she was an affectionate and deeply caring mother, I have no doubt that her unresolved trauma affected her mothering skills, particularly regarding emotional support and nurturing. In fact, the preceding sentence belies the conundrum I faced for many years: How could my mother be concurrently loving and emotionally neglectful? Although motherhood typically produces a range of challenges for most women, the impact of carrying unresolved trauma can be especially complex. Mothers are a child's first connection to the world, mothers who have experienced unresolved trauma often have difficulties creating the secure attachments with their child that are necessary for the child to feel safe. These mothers may experience difficulties soothing their children, responding to their children's needs, or mimicking their children's behaviours—all of which contribute to secure attachment (Sharma).

In my mother's case, her siblings' and relatives' violent deaths were never referred to, and although she occasionally discussed these siblings in the context of family events, such facts as the married name of her sister and details of siblings' partners were never mentioned. Over the years, other family members related (often conflicting) stories about their wartime experiences, yet my mother's silence and withdrawal when the subject was broached proved confusing and off-limits to me. Several trauma theorists including Dori Laub, Cathy Caruth, and Yael Danieli have identified the trauma victim's use of silence as both sanctuary and imprisonment to guard against unbearable reality (Laub, "Bearing Witness" 58, 69). The term "silent conspiracy" has frequently been used to describe the fear Holocaust survivors have in communicating their experiences, often to shield their children from the pain that they, the parents, endured. This may be done in the belief that their children will become more psychologically and emotionally robust (Lev-Wiesel). Arjan—a second-generation child herself—refers to a 2011 study, which highlights that such nonverbal communication created a higher level of secondary traumatic stress, suggesting that silence breeds stress. Arjan concludes that open, verbal communication in families with a legacy of trauma might mitigate symptoms of secondary traumatic stress.

Over the years, I have found comfort and reassurance in reading of those with similar experiences to my own. Arjan describes a cyclical "conspiracy of silence" and writes that many survivors did not want to speak about their experiences with their children, and the children did not want to question them for fear of causing further hurt (114). Arjan refers to common second-generational conversational responses, such as "'We didn't talk about it at home' or 'My father talked about it but not my mother'" (114). I could also identify with her description of how this silence affected the second generation, how we "absorbed the guilt, the fear, the shame and helplessness without having any direct access to those experiences or even to a meaningful frame of reference." (119). Another challenge I encountered, common to other children of survivors, was the issue of the ownership of memory: Did I have the right to grieve for family members I never knew or for experiences I did not encounter firsthand? The difficulty in finding a framework to address this meant that I could not do so until relatively recently, even with my siblings. My sister and I only recently discussed our feelings of shame, of feeling uncared for, and of being different to our peers. We both identified intuiting the message that we lived in a safe country, and whatever may happen to us could not compare to what our parents endured. We also acknowledged feeling the need to conceal any hardship or trouble we experienced to avoid provoking an hysterical reaction from our mother.

Regrettably, during adolescence, my reactions became somewhat hostile towards what I considered to be my mother's foibles. I responded to her often extreme reactions with silent disdain and shared little of my inner life or everyday events with her. Although I felt the need for rebellion, I did so quietly and always with an awareness of my parents' emotional fragility, of feeling that they could break. My silent rebellion took the form of an eating disorder accompanied by a depression that reemerged at other stages of my life.

## The Shift in Generations

As a young adult, I left my parents' home by marrying someone much older, with a paternal disposition that suited me at the time. As I matured and gained a stronger sense of self, the marriage failed. Soon after, I met my current partner and became pregnant. During pregnancy, I began to reassess my childhood, as many women do, and made pledges about the kind of mother I intended to be. My feelings towards my mother during pregnancy were ambivalent. At times, I hoped my child would enjoy a close bond with her grandmother just as I had with mine, and other times I judged her harshly for what I perceived to have missed out on as a child. My mother displayed anxieties during my pregnancy that appeared to reference past traumas; for example, she was keen for my partner and me to marry to avoid our child being victimized for being illegitimate (as had happened under national socialism). She was also opposed to our preference for the name Felix, should our child be male, for its German associations.

Towards the end of my pregnancy, it became clear that my mother was becoming increasingly ill. After experiencing a complicated birth, I longed for my mother to mother me through my own trauma, yet she was physically unable to even visit the hospital. Soon after, I learned that she was suffering terminal cancer, a fact that she had insisted on keeping from me until after the baby was born. This misguided decision—yet another conspiracy of silence—robbed me of the opportunity to grieve and adapt to the situation. I felt shut out, infantilized, and guilty for craving more family support while they were all focused on my mother. She died four months after my daughter's birth, and I tried my best to suppress feelings of abandonment—not too dissimilar from those of my childhood. I also mourned her loss on my daughter's behalf. I later learned that these feelings were not unique. D. L. Sheeran et al. write of one pregnant woman who had lost her mother to cancer and struggled through grief and loss in the transition to new motherhood. She related several moments when she realized that her absent mother would never be there to share all the moments of joy with her, nor could she pick up the phone to talk to her. Like me, she expressed deep grief in knowing how much her mother would have adored her baby (Sheeran et al.).

Although I did not succumb to postnatal depression (PND) immediately after giving birth, I suffered periods of depression over subsequent years that eventually became manageable through a combination of therapy and medication. This, I propose, is where the line between postmemory trauma and PND meet and blur. In her work on daughters becoming mothers, psychotherapist Anna Kinnaird-Folkman notes that studies of women's depression have found strong links between childhood adversity and depressive episodes in adulthood, whereas several studies have linked PND to how one was mothered. She refers to psychoanalyst Hedrika C Halberstadt-Freud's 1993 study that suggests PND "is caused by a woman's unresolved ties to her own mother: the woman who becomes a mother is strongly confronted with her inner mother or maternal image. In PND she mourns the mothering she missed" (419).

The intervening years have presented various challenges in parenting my two children; some occurred predictably during adolescence and others less so. Since recently becoming a grandmother, the cycle of postmemory trauma has again surfaced with new and unexpected tensions arising between my daughter and me. In becoming a mother, my daughter perpetuated the cycle of scrutinizing her childhood and revisiting unresolved feelings towards me. She struggled with remembrances of feeling unsupported and shut out, just as I had as a child. That I had unwittingly extended this intergenerational cycle was jolting, though not totally unpredictable. Kinnaird-Folkman describes the ambivalence of some new mothers who desire to reject their mother while clinging to her, wavering between love and hate. Further, Arjan suggests that the survivor's silence can extend into unintentional silencing of their descendants and the following generations, especially their grandchildren.

## The Role of Art in Working through Grief

My art practice has assisted me in working through conflicting feelings I have had around mothering. The links between art, mothering and melancholy have been considered by several theorists—from philosopher Roland Barthe's meditations on photographic representations of his mother in *Camera Lucida* to Julia Kristeva's linking of the mother figure, melancholia, and art in *Black Sun: Depression and Melancholia*. Artist Beverley Ayling-Smith refers to Kristeva's interpretation of melancholia as arising from an unsuccessful separation from the mother and posits that every artistic work, "even those geared to provoke a strong emotional response, is executed with a certain detachment" ("Connecting" 300). She surmises that this detachment enables the artist to incorporate aspects of their life into their work rather than representing their life; therefore, the work of art becomes a "physical manifestation of the artist's work of mourning—the work of art itself which is outside the body and can then be viewed by the spectator" (300). Although the artist may not experience bereavement and loss any more keenly than others, they possess the ability to use their work to share and communicate pain—making the private public (300). While agreeing with Ayling-Smith's views on the artist's distinctive capacity to communicate loss and bereavement, I would add that the immersive process in making art could also be viewed as a means for engaging with feelings of loss, absence, and trauma rather than actually representing these concepts. These embodied processes can often play an important role in unfolding meaning, creating space for contemplation, and the possibility of working towards reconciling grief. Artist Ann Hamilton's references to the labour of creating as a way of knowing has strong resonances to my own creative processes (Wallach). Her belief that the body leaves a transparent presence in the material also ties in with the materiality and physicality of the works I discuss below.

The choice of materials in creating artwork is imperative to the communication of the intention behind the work, be it as concept, metaphor, or narrative. Several artists have used textiles to communicate loss, trauma, and maternal relationships. Many of the works of Colombian artist Doris Salcedo for example, particularly the *Untitled* (1987–2008) series and *La Casa Viuda I* (1992–94), feature children's clothing and related objects to communicate trauma and absence. This clothing is often embedded within disproportionately sized, concrete-filled domestic timber furniture. The affective response to this contrast between delicately embroidered clothes and engulfing concrete jolts the viewer and encourages us—as is typical of Salcedo's work—to feel through the materiality. She balances the implied violence of the mutant furniture and concrete against the hints of human presence—often a child's dress or a fragment, such as a zipper.

My works *Hand in Hand* and *Unknitting/Rewind* both utilize textiles relevant to my mother and reimagined by me. *Hand in Hand* is a large floor installation inspired by an embroidered pillowcase from my mother's dowry collection, and *Unknitting/Rewind* metaphorically and literally unravels sixty years of memory in pulling apart then reknitting a cardigan knitted by my mother for my sister. For second-generation trauma survivors, such as myself, these objects are imbued with family connections that can take on heightened significance by standing in for their absent owners. Our daily interactions with these domestic textiles enable familiarity and intimacy; such textiles—bed sheets, clothes, knitted garments, etc.—enfold bodies and bear witness to life events. They often speak of domestic life and maternal links. This universal experience when encountering such materials in artworks evokes in the viewer a familiarity that crosses cultural boundaries (Ayling-Smith,

"The Bedsheet"). Artwork can also act as a catalyst for the viewer to remember through finding common shared life experiences or emotions and thus enable "a better understanding of the self" (15).

## Hand in Hand

The work *Hand in Hand* is an installation that reinterprets one of my mother's embroidered pillowcases. The work entails painstakingly arranging several hundred small stones onto my mother's tablecloth, which is laid out on a large, raised floor plinth. The pillowcase and tablecloth came from my mother's dowry collection that had remained largely untouched since her death, and the stones reference the Jewish memorial custom of leaving a stone on a loved one's grave. The linen was an integral part of our family life and informed my earliest childhood memories. I came to regard it not only as a link to my mother but as a connection to my family history and matrilineage. My mother's stitched monogram, WE (Weiss Eva), adorns almost every piece of this collection, from the table linen to bed linen, and can be regarded as both an indexical trace and material proof of her former existence. This linen, with its stains and creases from years of usage and storage, also offers the capacity to connect existentially to another person in another time. Historian Laurel T. Ulrich's references to the utilization of material goods to "create a world of meanings and ultimately transmit (her) history" resonated strongly for me, whereas remarks on material goods being "crucial props in unobserved, intimate rituals" brought to mind this ancient and comforting Jewish custom of leaving stones on graves (qtd. in Griffin 99).

The embroidered pattern of the pillowcase was recreated using one small quartz stone for each stitch. Thus, the entire installation period was spent with the folded pillowcase in hand, counting each stitch row by row and laboriously laying out each stone in a corresponding grid-like pattern. The monogram grew to almost four times the size of the original textile and took several arduous days to complete while being hunched on the floor over the work. It was physically and mentally challenging, testing my patience as well as my stamina, and I found myself addressing my mother aloud and expressing my frustrations, which added an unexpected yet realistic layer of meaning to the project.

## Unravelling

The video work and installation *Unknitting/Rewind* (2016) involved the unravelling then reknitting of a cardigan that had originally been knitted by my mother for my older sister almost sixty years earlier. It was handed down to me and then to my daughter. Although I regarded this cardigan as a link to my mother, it was also a testament to the significant connection to needlework in our matrilineal history. The decision to unpick the cardigan was made partly from my desire to unravel a history but also to reconnect with my mother by literally retracing her creative process, albeit in reverse. The embodied engagement I experienced in the unravelling process, and subsequent reknitting, similarly recalls the comfort of a common language. I was also mindful of Ann Hamilton's reference to how the rhythm of her hands in sewing recalled and reinforced distinct bodily memories reconnecting her to her grandmother (qtd. in Griffin).

It was then somewhat ironic that the experience once again proved to be at times frustrating. As is evident in the video, the unravelling—which, unedited, lasted a total of five hours—was torturously slow and emotionally challenging. In truth, it accurately reflected the ambivalent relationship I had experienced with my mother that has been evident in several other works I have made in reference to her. This need not be perceived as negative: In my need to create artwork in mourning for my mother, this artwork connected and resonated for me in a viscerally powerful way. In reknitting the cardigan, I mapped and faithfully followed the original pattern, deliberately allowing the wool to retain the memory of its earlier form, which resulted in a landscapelike, bumpy and textured, highly imperfect cardigan. The final work is presented as an eleven-minute looped video alongside the reknitted cardigan that is draped over the back of a chair.

*Unknitting/Rewind* was a transitional piece—my first artwork that has engaged with a past, intimate history to create new memories from old and to be passed on to future, female generations. Whereas *Hand in Hand,* and several other works paid homage to family connections, *Unknitting/Rewind* looks to the future, despite being an intimate work of mourning. Although these works could be regarded as grief work, they offer a form of resolution and demonstrate how engaging with personal objects, such as my mother's dowry linen, can enable a visceral sense of connection, which can be empowering. Such works can also engage the viewer and create a much-needed space for them to deal with their own grief and reflect on their own experiences.

## Works Cited

Arjan, G. *An Exploration of Resilience in the Generation after the Holocaust: Implications for Secondary Inheritors of Trauma, Displacement and Disastrous Events*. Dissertation. Taos Institute. Tilburg University, 2012.

Ayling-Smith, B. "Connecting with the Viewer: Affectivity and Cathexis in Textile Artwork." *Textile*, vol. 17, no. 3, 2019, pp. 296-311.

Ayling-Smith, B. "The Bedsheet: From Linen Cupboard to Art Gallery." *Textile*, vol. 16, no. 3, 2018, pp. 287-300.

Barthes, R. *Camera Lucida: Notes on Photography*. Hill and Wang, 1981.

Caruth, C. *Trauma: Explorations in Memory*. Baltimore: The Johns Hopkins University Press, 1995.

Griffin, S. *Inscribing Memory: Art and the Place of Personal Expressions of Grief in Memorial Culture*. Dissertation. Sydney, University of Sydney, 2016.

Hirsch, M. *The Generation of Postmemory: Writing and Visual Culture after the Holocaust*. Columbia University Press, 2012.

Hirsch, M. "Surviving Images: Holocaust Photographs and the Work of Postmemory." *The Yale Journal of Criticism*, vol. 14, no. 1, 2001, pp. 5-37.

Kinnaird-Folkman, A. "When Daughters Become Mothers: A transpersonal understanding of difficult postnatal feelings". *Living Therapy Counselling*, 2012, livingtherapycounselling.com/wp-content/uploads/2014/04/When-Daughters-Become-Mothers-A-transpersonal-understanding-of-difficult-postnatal-feelings.pdf Accessed 3 July 2022.

Kristeva, J. *Black Sun: Depression and Melancholia*. Columbia University Press, 1989.

Laub, D. "Bearing Witness or the Vicissitudes of Listening." *Testimony: Crises of Witnessing in Literature, Psychoanalysis, and History*, edited by Shoshana Feldman and Dori Laub, Routledge, 1992, pp. 57-74.

Laub, D., and D. Podell. "Art and Trauma." *The International Journal of Psychoanalysis*, vol. 76, 1995, pp. 991-1005.

Lev-Wiesel, R. "Intergenerational Transmission of Trauma across Three Generations: A Preliminary Study." *Qualitative Social Work*, vol. 6, no. 1, 2007, pp. 75-94.

Sharma, S. *Take Care of Me—But I Can't Right Then, I Have to Tend to my Daughter: The Influence of Mothers' Childhood Trauma on Parenting*. Dissertation. Faculty of The Chicago School of Professional Psychology, 2015.

Sheeran, D. L., et al. "Women's Relationships with their Own Mothers in the Early Motherhood Period." *International Journal of Gender and Women's Studies*, vol. 3, no. 1, 2015, pp. 26-32.

Wallach, A. "A Conversation with Ann Hamilton in Ohio." *American Art*, vol. 22, no. 1, 2008, pp. 51-77.

Chapter 11

# Her Face Is My Face, Too: Matrilineal Connection through Art Practice

Allegra Holmes

The feminist reclamation of both mothering and domestic practice through visual art has the potential to liberate not only the women of today but the memory of women who handed down these practices. Western society's attitude towards domestic work is one of insincere appreciation at best, and more usually, explicitly dismissive. The home is the forefront of feminist struggle, as it is within the home that culture and politics are intimately practiced and embedded in one's identity. If patriarchy is to maintain control, it is crucial that power structures be entrenched and upheld within the home. When women are tasked with the bulk of domestic labour, there is little to no time for anything else. And yet, women have always found ways to weave strength and dissidence into their lives, even if that life is one curtailed by oppression.

In this chapter, I examine the connections and relationships between the women in my family and trace my matrilineal line retrospectively from myself to my maternal great-grandmother. For me, this matrilineal connection is facilitated by the objects my foremothers made during their lives and have significantly affected my own practice as an artist, researcher, and mother. I assert that the limitless quality of visual art makes it a particularly suitable and valuable platform through which ideas of mothering and feminism can be explored and understood. By approaching the objects made by my foremothers as artworks,

I examine not only the feminist politics of the decorative arts, domestic work and mothering, but also the specifically matricentric feminist politics of this kind of work and its potential as empowering acts of feminist resistance. I bolster my claims with the writings of bell hooks, Margot Anne Kelley, and Thomas Knauer, furthering my assertion that women's creative work can be an empowering, connective force that spans generations.

As I am engaging with the work of Black theorists in this chapter, it is prudent that I acknowledge the significant differences between their histories and experiences and my own. In applying hooks's writing about her grandmother's quilting to my maternal ancestors' creative work, I seek to examine the commonalities in the creative practices of so many women living, working, and mothering under varied oppressive circumstances. It is undeniable that hooks, her foremothers, and their descendants continue to face hardships that I, and my ancestors, could not imagine. I am committed to being anti-racist in my work. I believe that engaging with the work of theorists, both Black and theorists of colour, is crucial. As hooks writes:

> When we, women of colour, began to tell white women that females were not a homogenous group, that we had to face the reality of racial difference, many white women stepped up to the plate. I'm a feminist in solidarity with white women today for that reason, because I saw these women grow in their willingness to open their minds and change the whole direction of feminist thought, writing and action. (15)

It is in this spirit that I engage with hooks's work.

Contemporary discourse surrounding maternal self-care is absurdly incongruous. The importance of self-care for mothers is emphasized as crucial to their ability to be better mothers and partners—not simply as something vital to their own mental, physical, and emotional health as human beings. Mainstream discourse advertises maternal self-care as solitary showers and baths. What is basic hygiene and privacy for the rest of society is portrayed as a luxury for mothers. In this context, a mother carving out time in her life to devote to creative work can be seen as ludicrously indulgent. The mother who decidedly takes time to cease attending to others and engage in art practice is actively resisting the model of patriarchal motherhood. Similarly, the mothers of the past who did not have the benefits of feminist theory and advancements, still sought ways to fulfil their creative needs. The power obtained by the creation and dispersing of an object is twofold: first, the transcendence of the mundane is made possible by the generative act of making something, and, second, the distributing of the object to loved ones is both an act of love and an affirmation of the maker's existence. In his book *Why We Quilt*, Thomas Knauer proposes that "The gift of a quilt is an act of love not because it involves sharing something that we have made, but because it is a request, an act of hope that despite distance, giver and recipient will remain connected" (104). For me, this brings to mind the cupboard in my mother's storage room, filled with crocheted doilies gifted from women both relatives in blood and love alone, most of which were sent from my family's homeland of Italy. My mother cannot part with these doilies; her reasoning is heartfelt and emotional: "Somebody made each one of these by hand." For my mother, a crocheted object conjures the memory of her own mother performing this same work. Throughout my childhood, my mother engaged in similar domestic creativity herself, gifting me with memories of her making. To engage in and witness this creative practice has meant that even a so-called anonymous maker is humanized. Even a nameless and faceless woman from time long past can be identified with through her creative work because as a maker, one knows what it is to work yarn or stitch thread.

Like my mother, when I look upon the pieces in her crocheted collection, I see not only the piece before me. My mind travels, through time and space, to the tiny Italian town from where my maternal line originates. I see women sitting together talking while their hands work almost automatically, crocheting the doilies that now reside in my mother's cupboard. Many of these doilies are wrapped in now-ancient plastic bags, with a handwritten note on a slip of paper stating the maker's name—names of women I will never meet, who died long before I was born. Yet they continue to exist through the pieces they gifted to my mother. Knauer states that to gift a made object guarantees a connection that transcends time and even death. Of quilts, he states "[Each one] evokes its maker, suggests her presence even if she is ultimately absent. In this light, it is not just the quilt that endures. The quilter, too, outlasts the constraints of time" (107).

Margot Anne Kelley also observes this transcendent quality in her essay "Sister's Choices": stating that "A quilt connects the lives of grandmother, mother and daughter, providing an opportunity for storytelling and a place to record domestic particulars, to artistically rework women's experiences" (51). This is true as well for crochet. For my family, crochet is the primary creative practice that connects us. The notion of recording evidence of oneself and creativity in a material object resonates here, as the women in my family—consciously or unconsciously—have crocheted themselves into their pieces, creating objects that hold the memory of them. My maternal great-grandmother Luisa Di Leo's *Swan Doily* is an amusingly ornate textile piece (Figure 1). It takes form as a six-pointed star, constructed of fine, white cotton yarn. Each point possesses a three-dimensional crocheted swan, which when stuffed with cotton balls stands erect, with their beaded beaks pointing triumphantly upwards.

Figure 1. Luisa Di Leo, *Swan Doily*, 1974. Cotton and plastic beading. Photograph by Ona Janzen.

Di Leo's *Swan Doily* is a comical, self-aware theatrical piece. It showcases not only the artist's skill and ingenuity, but also reveals her aesthetic preferences and personality. At the time Di Leo made this, it had been many years since she and her family had lived as refugees, after their home was bombed by Nazi soldiers. Upon her return to the ruins of what was once her house and village, it was likely Di Leo could not imagine a future in which she was crocheting a swan rimmed doily. Yet as they rebuilt their homes from the rubble, Di Leo crocheted lace edgings to adorn the broken pieces of stone. *Swan Doily* came some thirty years later, after the crochet edgings were disassembled to make larger pieces, and the house was properly rebuilt, after Di Leo's daughters had immigrated to Australia and the United States and became mothers themselves. The piece is drawn from the same well of hope and resilience that motivated Di Leo to decorate her ruined home with crocheted lace. Reflecting upon the history of Di Leo's creative practice brings forth a simple and unpretentious message: Creativity allows us to reclaim even a small aspect of our lives amid circumstances well beyond our control. *Swan Doily* communicates that life goes on and has carried Di Leo's spirit beyond her death.

In the last years of her life, Di Leo took on the task of crocheting a bedspread for each of her grandchildren. She died before she could finish, but afterwards, her eldest daughter's mother-in-law, Maria Falcone, took up the task and finished them. As a result, the bedspreads preserved not only Di Leo's love for her grandchildren but also the love shared for them by Falcone. Furthermore, the bedspreads preserve the relationship and love between Falcone and Di Leo themselves. Di Leo crocheted herself into the bedspreads. Falcone crocheted not only herself but also her memory and love for Di Leo. In a patriarchal society that positions women—particularly in-laws—in opposition to each other, Falcone's and Di Leo's unintentional collaborative bedspreads offer an alternative narrative. The objects created are more than expressions of maternal love. This origin story reveals the multifaceted connections present within a family, particularly the bonds between women. It is the creative product of two different matrilineal lines, connected by love and crochet. In this way, it can be reasoned that women's creative practice generates opportunities to transcend not only the mundanity of daily life but also the limitations imposed by patriarchal stereotypes. Creative practice is a gateway into empowerment because it requires the maker to connect to themselves, to examine their ideas and their techniques and ultimately to trust in their thinking and abilities.

This empowerment plays out in my own art making. In the late 1940s, Di Leo was preparing for her eldest daughter—my grandmother—Mafalda's first Holy Communion. They had now returned to the ruins of their small town, Colledimacine, and begun the task of rebuilding their home from the rubble. The war had prevented Mafalda and her peers from receiving this sacrament at the traditional age. For the Italian Catholic, religion and culture are inextricably entwined, to the point that despite my personal atheism, I still bring out my presepio—the nativity scene—each Christmas. Determined to give her daughter the rite of passage that was taken by war, Di Leo set out on foot to the neighbouring town of Palena to buy fabric to make a communion veil.

The walk to Palena is approximately eleven kilometres and would have taken about three hours each way. The fabric was tulle, a transparent, near weightless material—a small length, which does not seem worth the physical exertion of six hours on foot. I believe that for Di Leo this walk was not simply about the purchase of tulle; a veil is not crucial to the sacrament of communion, and most of the girls in the village would not have had one. For Di Leo, the veil symbolized something else, something entirely different to the virginity and purity that the Catholic church sees in it. For Di Leo, the veil represented everything that had been taken from her, her family, and her country by the war. It symbolized traditions and rituals that had been cast aside during the war years, when all energy was put into survival.

This story drives my ongoing artwork *The Walk to Palena* (Figure 2). Using eleven kilometres of white, four-ply mercerised cotton yarn, I have been crocheting a single, enormous doily for the last two years. Starting with a simple floral lace motif. I have continued to crochet from memory, creating each round, following no pattern. The doily travels with me; my two-hour train commute has become prime crochet time. As it grows, it has begun to spread out over me on the train like a blanket, becoming less convenient to transport and work on and much more visible to those looking on. In *Whip Your Hobby into Shape: Knitting, Feminism and Construction of Gender*, Alla Myzelev argues that to knit in public disrupts the binary opposition of private and public spaces. Myzelev goes on to state that breastfeeding—an activity that is usually prescribed as a private, intimate act—functions in the same way. I work on the *The Walk to Palena* in much the same way that

I breastfeed. I do it whenever and wherever I need. I crochet and breastfeed as much in public spaces as I do in private. I have done so while attending conferences, teaching and during class, on public transport, in waiting rooms, and at the homes of nearly everyone I have visited. In doing this, I continually cross the boundary between the personal, the private, the professional, and the public. To breastfeed and crochet in public is to rebel against the oppressive patriarchal ideals that mandate women be ashamed of their biology and creative practice. In this way, *The Walk to Palena* is not only a material manifestation of the physical and emotional enormity of Di Leo's walk and its personal significance but also an act of feminist anarchism. To crochet such a large, imposing piece in public is to claim that space and to assert oneself and one's work as worthy of being seen. In drawing a parallel between breastfeeding and crochet, the specifically matricentric politics of domestic creative work is revealed. To perform these domestic practices outside the home is to bring the domestic interior into the public space. This disrupts ideas of patriarchal propriety and creates a kind of public intimacy.

Figure 2. Allegra Holmes, (3750 metres into). *The Walk to Palena*, 2018—present. Cotton. Photograph courtesy of the artist.

In choosing to use eleven kilometres of yarn, I am emphasizing that the purpose of this work is not the finished object per se but the process of getting there. Unravelled, this length of yarn would stretch the distance between Colledimacine and Palena, mapping Di Leo's walk. This yarn has also become the thread that connects her to me. The practice of crochet is the common thread in both our lives, and I feel Di Leo with me when I do it. At this time of writing, I have used thirty-two balls of yarn and am four kilometres into my metaphoric walk. I have decided to amend the original plan of eleven kilometres of yarn and to make *The Walk to Palena* a permanent, ongoing artwork. I have exhibited the artwork at various stages of construction, using its unfinished status to draw out additional meaning that would not otherwise exist. Rather than viewing *The Walk to Palena* as an unfinished artwork, I choose to see it simply as young. It is at the beginning of its life, and its continual growth alongside myself as its maker reflects a multitude of meanings and discoveries. Just as Di Leo's walk was not about the veil, *The Walk to Palena* is not about a finished object. It is about the creative practice passed through generations, the unending nature of feminist work, and the ever-expanding quality of maternal love. To continue this piece for all the days of my life is to carry a literal thread with me, crocheted into a single object. This thread connects me not only to Luisa Di Leo but also to Maria Falcone (my paternal great-grandmother), Mafalda Di Coio (my maternal grandmother), Giuliana Giorgi (my paternal grandmother), and Maria Luisa Holmes (my mother). Each of these women crocheted; each of these women, however unconsciously, established an ongoing creative practice throughout their lives. The *Walk to Palena* extends beyond the story that inspired it and connects me to all my foremothers.

By treating Di Leo and Falcone's objects as artworks, I have been able to draw out meanings of love and connection as well as notions of feminist empowerment. Reading their crocheted pieces as artworks reveals the connective thread between my foremothers and illustrates the unwritten documentation of history that is held in practices traditionally viewed as feminine. These things, often referred to as women's work, are essential to life yet remain remarkably under-considered. Artist Rachel Epp-Buller describes the dismissive attitude to both artistic practices and academic research on topics related to the domestic space, stating, it is problematically assumed that "if one is making work related to the family it must surely be only about one's own family and not about any larger cultural issues" (9). By reframing the objects and techniques of my foremothers as art and highlighting their empowering facets, I am challenging the prevalent notion that domestic creative work is devoid of meaning.

In reclaiming my foremothers' creative works as art, I am reconceptualizing the history of domestic creative work as an art practice. This is a somewhat radical position, as it is antithetical to the conventional, patriarchal concept of the artist and art studio. Treating domestic creative practice as art reframes it as a method of feminist resistance and empowerment. Doing so retroactively empowers the memory of the women who passed down these creative traditions. My maternal line is filled with women who despite their varied oppressions were empowered to create. Their individual and combined practices have created a material legacy, in which meaning, material, and process are intertwined.

In "Aesthetic Inheritances: History Worked by Hand," hooks discusses quilting as a reclamation of a woman's time. She writes of her grandmother's quilting practice: "Quilt-making was a spiritual process where one learned to surrender. It was a form of meditation where the self was let go. This was the way she had learned to approach quilt-making from her mother. To her, it was an art of stillness and concentration, a work which renewed the spirit" (53).

The early quilts made by hooks's grandmother were composed of scraps and were vitally necessary for the family to keep warm–to survive. The making of these quilts can be viewed as selfless acts of devotion, the giving up of one's time and utilizing one's skills for the benefit of the family. While this aspect cannot be denied, hooks further elucidates that the practice of quilting created a space in which her grandmother could cease attending to others and "come back to herself" (53). This reveals both the paradox and multidimensionality of mothers' creative work, where making both encompasses and transcends the orthodoxy of utility, devotion, maternal love and the reasons for creating. As much as hooks's grandmother's quilts and my foremothers' crocheted pieces were for the family, the making of these objects fulfilled something else within the women making them. To take ownership of one's time and use it to create is an act of defiance. For hooks's grandmother, it was to rail against the history of slavery and the legacy that filled her life with constant work. For my foremothers, it was to reclaim the joy and freedom stolen from them by both patriarchy and the World War. For myself, it is resisting the rules of patriarchal intensive motherhood, which demands that a mother's life and identity be entirely consumed by acts of service to the family as well as the rules of the patriarchal art world, which demand that the artist's life and identity be entirely consumed by devotion to their work. In holding the supposedly opposing identities of mother and artist as central to myself and allowing them to overlap and intertwine, I am resisting patriarchal control.

Redefining *The Walk to Palena* as a permanent ongoing artwork is also an exercise in hope for my own life. It is an exercise of looking forwards and of imagining and investing in a future. My nonni (grandparents) and their contemporaries have a saying: "Ho fatto la Guerra." This translates to "I did the war," and they would say it in response to any hardship, big or small. When they say it, they mean "If I have to, I can face anything." I have heard the war stories of my nonni, told from their perspectives as children and teenagers. I have cried, I have marvelled, and I have felt pride in the people I came from and deep sorrow for all those that suffered. After having my own children, I began to reflect on these stories from the maternal perspective, what it must have been like for Di Leo to see her daughters' future dissolve before her eyes. Di Leo saw her house bombed. She ran from bullets with her young daughters. She crossed a river to escape Nazi occupation, and she lived with her family as a refugee before returning to her destroyed hometown. Alongside the rebuilding of houses and communities, I believe that Luisa's walk to Palena was a way to rebuild herself and to reclaim her sense of safety and freedom. Creating *The Walk to Palena* makes Di Leo an active presence in my daily life. Luisa Di Leo died long before I was born, and yet I have felt deeply connected to her all my life. I cannot remember a time when her daughter, my Nonna Mafalda, was not telling me "Hai la faccia di mia madre" ("You have my mother's face). I grew up knowing that her face is mine, too.

## Works Cited

Epp Buller, Rachel. "Performing the Breastfeeding Body: Lactivism and Art Interventions." *Studies in the Maternal*, vol. 8, no. 14, 2016, pp. 1-15.

hooks, bell. "Aesthetic Inheritances: History Worked by Hand." *Belonging: A Culture of Place*. Routledge, 2009.

Kelley, Margot Anne. "Sisters' Choices." *Quilt Culture: Tracing the Pattern*, edited by Judy Elsey and Cheryl B. Tornsey, University of Missouri Press, 1994.

Knauer, Thomas. *Why We Quilt: Contemporary Makers Speak out about the Power of Art, Activism, Community and Creativity*. Storey Publishing, 2019.

Myzelev, Alla. "Whip Your Hobby into Shape: Knitting, Feminism and Construction of Gender." *Textile: The Journal of Cloth and Culture*, vol. 7, no. 2, 2009, pp. 148-63.

Chapter 12

# Minding the Mother: Intrapsychic Effects of the Mother-Daughter Relationship in Elena Ferrante's *The Lost Daughter*

Inês Faro

*The Lost Daughter*, originally published in Italian in 2006 under the name *La figlia oscura*, is Elena Ferrante's third novel. Elena Ferrante is the pseudonym of the contemporary Italian writer who has devoted most of her work to the representation and the exploration of the mother-daughter relationship in contemporary Italian society. In this novel, the author challenges the normative notions of mothers' and daughters' subjectivities in the Italian literary landscape.

The majority of reviews of *The Lost Daughter* highlights how the story focuses on Leda, typically described as a bad mother, who has abandoned her daughters when they were young, and who, years later, mysteriously becomes obsessed with a girl's doll while spending her summer break on a beach in Southern Italy. In this chapter, I propose a different approach to the novel by refusing to categorize Leda as a "bad mother" and by elaborating on her complex relationship with both her mother and daughters. I argue that *The Lost Daughter* explores the experience of motherhood as one of connection and separation (Hirsch 6) from one's mother. I examine the mechanics of the text to support the idea that Leda's relationship with her mother is the point of reference in her attempt at negotiating her subjective configuration as a woman and a mother of two young women. To do so, I focus on Leda's mother's omnipresent voice throughout the text via Leda's intrapsychic dialogues with both her mother and her daughters and via her projections and reactions towards a mother-daughter-doll (mother-daughter-baby) trio she encounters during the summer break.

## Red Flags

In the opening lines of *The Lost Daughter*, Leda, a middle-aged professor of literature, suddenly feels ill while driving from the Ionian coast in southern Italy where she had just spent her summer break. The illness, we learn some lines later, results from a serious injury on her left side —"an inexplicable lesion" (Ferrante 10). She forgets that she is driving and has the impression of being at the sea in the middle of the day: "The beach was empty, the water calm, but on a pole a few meters from shore a red flag was waving" (10). Recurrent throughout the novel, this "seasickness," or sense of being dislocated, hints at her experience as a young girl, as a daughter, and as a mother. Her fantasy of being at the beach in which a red flag is waving triggers the first internal dialogue with her mother. It also prepares the reader for her mother's omnipresent voice throughout the text. Leda remembers being a child and her mother instructing her to never go swimming if there was a red flag: "It means the sea is rough and you might drown" (10). The advice sounds reasonable. However, the repercussions of this memory while she is driving unveils something more fundamental about Leda's relationship with her mother: her need to be freed from her mother's frightening projections. As an old presage haunting her, Leda recalls how fearful she used to feel about being near the water. She recounts when she was near the shore and how her mother would appear and ask "Leda, what are you doing, don't you see the red flag?" (10). Leda's fear of red flags as a young child had led her into a state of suspended agency. She would remain "on the shore, cautiously testing the water with the tip of [her] toe" (9). We are invited to think about "red flags" as a metaphor in Leda's narrative economy, particularly how red flags allude to how her relationship with her mother impacted her development as a woman and as a mother. The effects of this relationship can also be explored as a metonym: Red flags can stand for the cultural, normative flags waved by her maternal lineage and by Italian society for women, specifically mothers.

## Mother-Daughter Dyad

Psychoanalysis is one of the fields that recognizes how the construction of female subjectivity is inevitably related to the experience of having been daughtered by a mother or by a maternal figure. It is now acknowledged that the affirmation of a woman's existence happens in an ongoing dialogue with the mother throughout life. This idea clashes with a rather unidirectional conception developed in the early days of psychoanalysis. Freud's statements on female development and his phallocentric views to explain the girl's change of libidinal object from mother to father, implied that to become an adult, women need first to separate from the mother to be closer to the father. Following the feminist deconstructions of psychoanalytic considerations about the figure and role of the mother, the mother-daughter relationship has been redefined. French psychoanalyst Luce Irigaray posits that the mother cannot, and should not, be excluded from women's psychosexual and psychosocial development. In the late 1970s, the sociologist and psychoanalyst Nancy Chodorow proposed that women's identity is interconnected and indistinguishable from the relationship a woman has with her mother. Chodorow's work is relevant to this day, for it refigures our understanding of female subjectivity as dynamic and cyclical, evocative of Demeter and Persephone's tale. Other authors have enhanced the interactive and dialectical process between mother and daughter across their lifespan. Paula Bernstein, for instance, argues that on each developmental step, women dialogue in thought or reality with their mothers. Again, female (and male) development is not seen as one that evolves towards separation but is construed as a dynamic and relational process throughout the lifecycle. The child and adolescent psychoanalyst E. Kirsten Dhal argues as follows:

> The process of psychic integration of the tie to the mother as an aspect of the self is never fully complete. The hallmark of adult female psychic organization lies in the daughter's capacity to permit continuing reverberations within herself of the representations of the tie to the mother in her ongoing intrapsychic dialogue with her mother. (201-02)

Being engaged in a lifelong exchange (intrapsychic or real) with the mother is thus necessary for a woman's mental health and development and ought not to be pathologized. This idea is also endorsed by the psychoanalysts Robert Emde and Helen Buchsbaum, who propose that, ideally, a women's development would be towards autonomy with connectedness with the mother. They suggest that "the connected feeling is not regressive; it is essential to superego development and to the feeling of mastery that supports autonomy" (608). Being in dialogue with the mother either through identification with her good parts or via a disidentification with the bad parts is thus a fundamental basis for the constitution of the subject.

The theoretical shift from the need to separate to be able to individuate towards a more back-and-forth way of achieving maturity in women is of great relevance to help us think about Leda's internal dialogue with her mother and the effects of that ongoing dialogue in her relationship with a Neapolitan mother-daughter-doll trio at the beach. This idea gains significance if we add how Leda's experience as a mother of two girls is mediated, behaviourally and linguistically, by the experiences she had with her mother. Leda's ambivalent reactions to the people around her, particularly to other women, and the actualization of her mother's threats in her relationship with her daughters expose the long-term impact of her relationship with her (real and fantasied) mother. Simultaneously, her ambivalence uncovers her difficult, painful, guilt-inducing fight against the submission to an angry or mute maternal lineage.

## Ancestors in the Flesh

The second chapter is the beginning of the story in time. Leda is alone for the first time in twenty-five years. Her two daughters, both in their twenties, have moved to Canada to live with their father. She decides to go on a vacation to the south of Italy. On her way, she feels anxious and recalls how she used to worry about her daughters' wellbeing: "I was afraid they would accuse me of being what in fact I was, distracted or absent, absorbed in myself" (Ferrante 13). While in the house she rents near the sea, she notices a cicada on her pillow and comments on how the "stomach of the females doesn't have elastic membranes, it doesn't sing, it's mute" (14). She opens the window and tosses the insect out.

This scene of her getting rid of the silent female insect hints at Leda's struggle with her silence.

In the following chapters, the summer goes by, and she settles into a routine of swimming, writing, and preparing the next academic year. The colour of the pine nuts evokes memories and becomes pretexts for her to reengage in intrapsychic dialogues with her mother and with her daughters. She feels at peace and no longer "a burden to [her]self" (17). At the beach, she notices a loud family of Neapolitans—"a large family group, similar to the one I had been part of when I was a girl, the same jokes, the same sentimentality, the same rages" (18). Some days later while she is reading, she notices as part of the group a young mother, Nina, her daughter, Elena, and the girl's doll, Nani. This mother, she tells us, looks like "an anomaly in the group, an organism that had mysteriously escaped the rule, the victim, now assimilated, of a kidnapping or of an exchange in the cradle" (18). The idea of a person as an anomaly in the group and as an assimilated victim from an alien environment alludes to Leda's self-representation as inadequate and an outcast within her family and society. She later describes the girl: "There was something off about the little girl, I don't know what; a childish sadness, perhaps, or a silent illness. Her whole face expressed a permanent request to her mother that they stay together: it was an entreaty without tears or tantrums, which the mother did not evade" (18-19). The daughter's dependency and the mother's attentiveness to her daughter's needs disturb Leda. She becomes absorbed in the dynamics between the triangle formed by the mother-daughter-doll at the beach. She notices the tenderness, and the pleasure they take in their togetherness: "They laughed together, enjoying the feeling of body against body, touching noises, spitting out streams of water, kissing each other ... in her motherhood there was something that distinguished her; she seemed to have no desire for anything but her child" (19). She describes how the mother talks to her daughter and to the doll in the "pleasing cadence" (20) of the Neapolitan dialect, which Leda associates with the enjoyable part of her childhood—"the language of playfulness and sweet nothings" (20). Simultaneously, she is reminded of its nastiest parts: "I remember the dialect on my mother's lips when she lost that gentle cadence and yelled at us, poisoned by her unhappiness" (21). Leda recalls her mother's threats to leave her children and how she used to say: "I can't take you anymore,

I can't take any more" (21). "In reality," she says, "[the mother] was there, in her words she was constantly disappearing from home" (21). The contrast of her experience and the tenderness between mother, Nina, daughter, Elena, and the doll is at the origin of Leda's shift from contemplation to envy. Seeing them playing irritates her and quickly "becomes an unbearable pain" (23).

In the next scene, Leda walks through the bushes. Suddenly, a violent blow strikes her back. She sees a pinecone and later at home she identifies on her body "the sticky traces of resin" (31). Leda feels a pain, however, but she feels at a loss about the origin: "I couldn't decide if the pinecone had been thrown deliberately from the bushes or had fallen from a tree" (31). Her doubt about the source of her pain suggests her difficulty in understanding what she has done deliberately in her life and what, on the contrary, had simply "fallen" from her (family) tree. In this sense, the traces of resin can be interpreted as her perception of the viscous, adhesive quality of her origins. This idea seems to be confirmed, when some pages later, there is another reference to how genealogy shapes bodies and minds. Leda says: "One looks at a child and immediately the game of resemblances begins, as one hurries to enclose that child within the known perimeter of the parents. In fact, it's just live matter, yet another random bit of flesh descended from long chains of organisms" (36). She further explores the weight of genealogy when she describes Elena, the youngest of the Neapolitan clan, at the beach: "I watched the child, but, seeing her like that, alone and yet with all her ancestors compressed into her flesh, I felt something like repugnance, even though I didn't know what repelled me" (37). Like Elena, Leda is alone at the beach and yet, in her female body and mind can also be found the "chain of mute or angry [Neapolitan] women [she] came from" (64).

## The Lost Daughters

Later in the novel, Leda sees Elena's mother and the family mad with anxiety looking for Elena, who has temporarily disappeared on the beach. Leda reflects:

> A child who gets lost on the beach sees everything unchanged and yet no longer recognizes anything. She is without orientation

.... The child feels that she is exactly where she was and yet doesn't know where she is ... everything or person is alien to her and so she cries. To the unknown adult who asks her what's wrong, why she is crying, she doesn't say that she's lost, she says that she can't find her mama. (41-42)

Once again, the scene will evoke painful memories related with her mother. Leda recalls her experience of feeling lost as a child and echoes her own feelings of distress and emotional deregulation. The loss she is alluding to is also metaphorical, it refers to her attachment to the damaged relationship with her mother: "I was afraid that it was my mother who would get lost, I lived in the anxiety of not being able to find her" (40). Leda's fantasy and anxiety suggest a failure in the intersubjective dynamics in the mother-daughter dyad and the "violation of expected patterns of soothing or responsiveness" from mother to daughter (Benjamin 6). The ongoing dialogue with her mother throughout the novel reflects Leda's quest for a mother who would have taken care of her and guided her in the moments in which she felt lost. This hypothesis is later confirmed when she expresses the rejection her mother made her feel: "I had been certain that my mother, in creating me, had separated herself from me, as when one has an impulse of revulsion, and, with a gesture, pushes away the plate" (Ferrante 58). The impact of Leda's perception of mother's separation from her is lifelong. It also influences Leda's relationship with her daughters, as illustrated through Leda's ambivalence as the result of the enduring negotiation of separation and attachment between her and her girls.

## Doll: To Flesh Out the Pain

Leda's account of her uneasiness and irritation with Elena's doll appears early on in the novel, when she watches the mother and daughter playing together and speaking to the doll, "superimposing the adult's fake-child voice and the child's fake-adult voice" (22). Halfway through the holidays, she sees the doll, "abandoned in the sand, limbs askew, her face half buried, as if she was about to suffocate" (45). Leda picks it up, and although she feels that she has done something "mean" (45), she decides to keep the doll. This gesture will painfully activate memories and confront her with her rawest feelings.

The "ugly old doll" (38) will allow for a doubled mediation of Leda's experience of being a daughter and a mother. By stealing the doll, Leda swaps places with Elena. The child becomes suddenly overwhelmed, and the adult gives herself a time to play. Leda has in the doll a chance to negotiate her identity as well as an opportunity to confront her internal breaches. "Mammucia," a "word for doll that hasn't been used for a long time" also means a mother substitute, becomes a transitional space, an intermediate area of experience (Winnicott 46). It enables Leda to confront her early experiences involving her body, as a daughter, as a pregnant woman, and as a mother to her daughters. The doll thus functions as a space to think and to embody maternal subjectivity: to birth, to mother, to care, to hate, to abject, and to sexualize are all refigured as subjective processes through the figure of the doll (Elwell).

The doll also allows for the bridging between Leda's intrapsychic space and her genealogical spaces. The water that trickles from the mouth of the doll in Leda's bathroom sink reminds her of her first pregnancy. She recalls how during that time she felt unique and different from the other women in the family: "I was not my grandmother, I was not my mother, I was not my aunts, my cousins. I was different and rebellious ... I imagined myself a shining tile in the mosaic of the future" (122). While pregnant, Leda was what René Kaës defines as an "intersubject" (238)—a subject "divided between the demands imposed on him by the necessity of serving his own purposes and those that derive from his status and function as a member of an intersubjective chain, of which he is at one and the same time the servant, the link of transmission, the heir, and the actor" (241). Contrary to what happened to the women in her family who "swelled, dilated" (Ferrante 122) and with whom "the creature trapped in their wombs seemed a long illness that changed them," Leda wanted instead her pregnancy "to be under control" (122). It is a desire that she reenacts all these years later in the play with the doll.

The doll as a pregnant woman is the figure of a transitional body that articulates different voices and that becomes indeed the voice and the body of superimposed generations. This unique condition is relieved through the water leaving the body of the doll, which alludes to the amniotic fluid and vomiting during pregnancy and to the fluids that are expulsed in childbirth, together with the baby. In that sense, the doll becomes a privileged space for an eventual process of mourning and reparation. The slime that comes out of the doll's mouth brings to mind what she refers to as the "destructive energy in [her] belly" (78). The anger Leda used to feel towards her daughters and towards her mother is now relocated in the "liquid darkness" (100) in the doll's stomach—a darkness that she wants to eviscerate from herself. The catharsis of this game takes place when a worm is expelled from the viscera of the doll. The satisfaction Leda takes in this expulsion evokes the internal worms that she wants out of her psyche: guilt, envy, hate, as well as the weight of the past. However, when the doll finally finishes with the vomiting, Leda fantasizes the doll's womb as a dry ditch. That image leads her to think: "Organize, understand. I thought how one opaque action generates others of increasingly pronounced opacity, and so the problem is to break the chain" (128). The novel leaves us with an unanswered question: Is it possible to ever break free from the impact of one's experience with her mother and from the cultural beliefs about how a mother-daughter relationship should be?

In the last pages of the novel, Leda is still at her holiday home. She has returned the doll to the mother of the child and receives a phone call from her daughters. Mimicking their mother's Neapolitan accent, the daughters ask: "what are you doing? ... Won't you at least let us know if you're alive or dead?" To which she answers: "I'm dead, but I'm fine" (140). Note that from the two options that her daughters gave her, she chooses "I am dead," probably in contrast with the feeling of being alive while she was in possession of the doll. Through her experience of the evisceration of the doll's body, Leda was confronted with the threat of disintegration, but she survived. On her way back home, she drives off the road. Once again, she keeps on living. As she tells us at the beginning of the novel, she cannot make sense of what just happened: "The hardest things to talk about are the ones we ourselves can't understand" (10). She chooses to keep her pain to herself and not to speak about the accident to anyone; however, the aftermath of her actions is not yet known.

## Works Cited

Benjamin, Jessica. *Beyond Doer and Done to. Recognition Theory, Intersubjectivity and the Third*. Routledge, 2018.

Bernstein, Paula. "Mothers and Daughters from Today's Psychoanalytic Perspective." *Psychoanalytic Inquiry*, vol. 24, no. 5, 2004, 601-28.

Chodorow, Nancy. *The Reproduction of Mothering: Psychoanalysis and the Sociology of Gender*. University of California Press, 1978.

Dahl, E. Kirsten. "Daughters and Mothers: Aspects of the Representational World During Adolescence." *Psychoanalytic Study of the Child*, vol. 50, 1995, pp. 187-204.

Elwell, Leslie. "Breaking Bonds: Refiguring Maternity in Elena Ferrante's *The Lost Daughter*." *The Works of Elena Ferrante*, edited by Grace Russo Bullaro and Stephanie Love, Palgrave Macmillan, 2016, pp. 237-69.

Emde, Robert N., and Helen K. Buchsbaum. "'Didn't You Hear My Mommy?' Autonomy with Connectedness in Moral Self-Emergence." *The John D. and Catherine T. MacArthur Foundation Series on Mental Health and Development. The Self in Transition: Infancy to Childhood*, edited by D. Cicchetti and M. Beeghly, University of Chicago Press, 1990, pp. 35-60.

Ferrante, Elena. *The Lost Daughter*. Translated by Ann Goldstein. Europa Editions, 2006.

Freud, Sigmund. "The Infantile Genital Organization (An Interpolation into the Theory of Sexuality)." *The Standard Edition of the Complete Psychological Works of Sigmund Freud, Volume XIX (1923-1925): The Ego and the Id and Other Works*, 1923, pp. 139-146.

Freud, Sigmund. "Female Sexuality." *The Standard Edition of the Complete Psychological Works of Sigmund Freud, Volume XXI (1927-1931): The Future of an Illusion, Civilization and its Discontents, and Other Works*, 1931, pp. 221-244.

Hirsch, Marianne. *The Mother/Daughter Plot, Narrative, Psychoanalysis, Feminism*. Indiana University Press, 1989.

Irigaray, Luce. *The Speculum of the Other Woman*. Translated by Gillian C. Gill. Cornell University Press, 1985.

Kaës, René. *Linking, Alliances, and Shared Space: Groups and the Psychoanalyst*. International Psychoanalytic Association, 2007.

Winnicott, Donald. "Transitional Objects and Transitional Phenomena —A Study of the First Not-Me Possession." *International Journal of Psycho-Analysis*, vol. 34, 1953, pp. 89-97.

Chapter 13

# Hija eres y madre serás: Daughters and Their Mothers in Latinx Memoirs by Cherríe Moraga and Anika Fajardo

Astrid Lorena Ochoa Campo

Memoir writing has been an important tool of visibility for Latinx authors. According to Norma E. Cantú, memoir writing is a political act: "Writing personal memoirs or autobiography constitutes an exercise in communal storytelling insofar as many of our stories cut across age, geography, and even gender and tell a shared story of injustice and prejudice" (320). The memoirs examined in this chapter, *Native Country of the Heart* by Cherríe Moraga and *Magical Realism for Non-Believers* by Anika Fajardo, focus on the intricate and often challenging family relationships in transnational contexts; respectively, they refer to their Chicano and Colombian communities in the United States (US). Although both communities are still marginalized in the US, in terms of the literary landscape, the first enjoys more recognition while the second is still emerging. These matrifocal narratives, read through an empathy studies lens, offer many insights about the influences of mothers in their daughters' lives as these have children of their own. Thus, I argue that as the protagonists, who are mothers, reflect on their relationships with their own mothers and the impact on their lives, they underscore empathy for the difficulties and struggles their mothers faced as women in foreign lands. Therefore, these memoirs also deal with issues of race, gender, class, and migration within the lived experiences of mothers and daughters who become mothers themselves.

Since the publication of such seminal works as *Of Woman Born* by Adrienne Rich, *My Mother/My Self* by Nancy Friday, and *The Reproduction of Mothering* by Nancy Chodorow, the relationship between mothers and daughters has been explored in a variety of writings. How this bond is perceived has also evolved, mostly from a focus on subtle or overt blame to reconciliatory attitudes. For example, in *Contemporary Chicana Literature: (Re) Writing the Maternal Script*, Cristina Herrera maintains that "Chicana writers are actively engaged in the process of rewriting motherhood," not only by "contesting the image of the static, disempowered Chicana mother" but also by offering "representations of Chicana mother-daughter relationships that are not merely a source of conflict but also a means through which both mothers and daughters may achieve agency" (13). US Colombian writers also lean towards more conciliatory mother-daughter relationships. Regarding this representation in *Vida*, a groundbreaking fictional work by US Colombian author Patricia Engel, Catalina Esguerra points out that the rebelliousness enacted by the young protagonist shows her "to be *more* like her mother" because both of them reject the norms of the elite circles to which they belong (359). In this sense, Esguerra's observation highlights the ways in which daughters unwittingly imitate mothers while thinking of themselves as radically different.

This imitation can manifest sometimes when daughters become mothers. For instance, Friday asserts in the new introduction of her book that for a daughter "motherhood brings a feeling of being reunited." She continues: "There can be even a kind of forgiveness of her own mother when she repeats with her daughter the very things she didn't like as a child—mother's nagging, mother's overprotectiveness" (xv). As the Spanish portion of this chapter's title reminds us, "now a daughter, later a mother," there are aspects of mothers' actions that are better understood by daughters when they go through similar experiences themselves. As I proceed to demonstrate, this turn towards empathy is manifested in the portrayal of mother-daughter relationships in the memoirs by Moraga and Fajardo.

## Empathy

The concept of empathy has generated considerable attention in recent decades in various disciplines. Sigrid Weigel even affirms that, today, empathy "is one of the hottest topics of research" (2). However, any approach to the study of empathy recognizes the difficult task of providing a precise definition of the term. It is generally recognized as being social (Hunt), emotional (Oatley), and that it can be improved with practice (Morson). From the neurobiological point of view, "the majority of the field perceives empathy as a human skill of perceived (inter) action, as the capacity for understanding the actions of others—and in this way somehow also their intentions" (Weigel 7). The history of the term shows that it was originally used in the artistic field and gradually its meaning was modified through disciplines. Today, the term empathy is understood as our ability to capture and understand the mental and emotional state of other people (Lanzoni 3). Hence, we are often invited to put ourselves in someone else's shoes—to understand their situation.

In this chapter, I use the conceptualization proposed by Amy Coplan, informed by recent studies in psychology and neuroscience. She defines empathy as "a complex imaginative process in which an observer simulates another person's situated psychological states while maintaining clear self-other differentiation" (5). This complex process has three essential characteristics: "affective matching, other-oriented perspective-taking, and self-other differentiation" (Coplan 6). According to Coplan, for affective matching to exist, it is necessary for the observer to experience the same type of emotions as those of the observed person (6). The next aspect, other-oriented perspective taking, differentiates empathy from simple emotional contagion insofar as it is a mediated activity in which one person constructs the subjective experience of another by simulating it from the point of view of this other person (Coplan 9). Most of the time, as I mentioned earlier, we are asked to put ourselves in the place of others, which is self-oriented because it involves imagining what we would do if we were in the place of the other person (Coplan 9). In this regard, Coplan clarifies the following: "In other-oriented perspective-taking, when I successfully adopt the target's perspective, I imagine being the target undergoing the target's experiences rather than imagining being myself undergoing the target's experiences" (13). Self-other differentiation allows us to be aware of the boundaries between our being and that of another person: "It allows the optimal level of distance from the other for successful empathy. We are neither fused nor detached. We relate to the other as an other but share in the other's experience in a way that bridges but does not eliminate the gap between our experiences" (Coplan 16). Aspects of the complex imaginative process explained by Coplan can be observed in the memoirs by Moraga and Fajardo. As the protagonists narrate their stories of family relationships, and the mother-daughter relationship in particular, they exhibit affective matching when they become mothers and are able to consider the perspective of their mothers while maintaining a clear sense of themselves.

## Remembering Mother

Moraga's memoir pays homage to her mother Elvira and their Mexican ancestors. The "native" part of her title refers to her efforts to reclaim their indigenous heritage on her mother's side. According to her daughter, Elvira was a strong woman who was always "present" (48). One of her main tasks was to "sow and hoe and grow us with a Mexican heart in an AngloAmerica that had already occupied the village" (49). Thus, Moraga's guidance in motherhood comes from her Mexican culture. One of the aspects she observes with curiosity is her mother's connection with the spirit world. From watching her mother pray to San Antonio to deliver her from cancer to maintaining an altar at her house, Moraga's childhood is imbued with her mother's spirituality, though not necessarily religiosity. This familiarity comes in handy later when Moraga has complications during the delivery of her son, Rafael Ángel.

In the chapter "Old School," Moraga writes: "At the age of forty, I became pregnant upon my first attempt at a home-based insemination" (104). As if by luck or fate, her water broke while she was visiting her parents in San Gabriel, California. Her premature son was born a week later and soon after "contracted a life-threatening intestinal infection fairly common among preemies" (105). The surgeries Moraga's son needed to undergo and her entrusting herself to goddesses remind her of her desperation when she would pray that her mother not die of cancer. However, she realizes the following: "I was no longer a child, but the *mother* of a child, who desperately needed me to be wholly present at that moment. There was no 'god' in such fear" (105). Just as her mother was always present, Moraga feels compelled to be the same for her son. Feeling the anguish for the wellbeing of her son allows Moraga to experience an affective matching now that she is a mother rather than a child. Moreover, when she finds herself "echoing my mother's words aloud, words she would repeat each time she entreated her santos [saints], lighting la veladora [candle] on her altar. *If it is God's will ... con el favor de Dios,*" she concludes that "we can control very little in this life, she knew, much better than I. And ultimately, we *are* in 'god's' hands" (106). During this vulnerable moment, Moraga looks at the situation from the perspective of her mother and, as she admits, would thank her mother "twelve years down the road" (106). Through the near-death experience of her son, Moraga comes to appreciate the lessons of surrender she learned from her mother: "I would walk alone or I would walk with she who could walk fearlessly in the face of death" (106). Mother and daughter remain close—but not fused—because of Moraga's assertion of her sexuality and freedom to choose her life. Although the mother worried about the choices her daughter made, the latter insisted on not "pretending we were other than who we are" (85). This emphasis on self-other differentiation creates the space to exercise empathy towards her mother even until her last days living with Alzheimer's disease. Elvira's recognition of her daughter in old age while struggling with an illness that affects memory eases the pain of Moraga, who appreciated that "she always remembered 'mi'ja'" even when her mother could not remember her name (166). The strength of the mother-daughter bond depicted in this memoir speaks of a daughter who through empathy is able to understand the life lessons learned from her mother's lived experience.

## Searching for Father, Understanding Mother

In her debut memoir, Fajardo tells the story of reconnecting with her Colombian father and discovering the existence of a half-brother she did not know about. However, having been raised by her mother and maternal grandparents, her reflections often revolve around her relationship with her American mother. Born in Colombia and raised in Minnesota, Fajardo revisits her family history from the perspective of both parents to grapple with the conflicting aspects of her identity;

for example, the fact she was "Colombian. But without a Colombian passport" (153). As Fajardo narrates her recollections from two visits to Colombia to meet up with her father, she tells the details she learns about the relationship between her parents and the reasons she grew up in the US with a single mother.

Nancy, Fajardo's mother, had studied abroad in Colombia, where she met Renzo, an aspiring artist. She was a teenager and quickly fell in love with the dashing Colombian. They married and had a daughter. However, their relationship quickly deteriorated due to Renzo's infidelities and subtle abandonment of his wife. So a few months into her pregnancy she left him to stay in another Colombian city with some of her friends. Fajardo humbly expresses her inability to fully comprehend what it must have been for her mother to make this choice: "When she had first arrived in Colombia, she had wanted to reinvent herself; now she would do it again. I would never completely understand what it had been like for her" (109). Eventually, Nancy could not stand the loneliness of raising a toddler almost by herself in a country where she did not fully belong. With the pretense to visit her parents, the family travels to Minnesota. There she executes the plan she had carefully crafted to keep her daughter in the US. She disappears with her, leaving Renzo with no way to fight for his daughter's custody and no other choice but to return to Colombia empty handed. Although with time Renzo and his daughter keep occasional communication, Fajardo grows up resenting her mother's decision to separate her from her dad.

As an adult, when Fajardo learns she is pregnant with her first child, she tries to imagine what her mother must have felt upon the realization of her pregnancy: "I pictured my mother reading her book on childbirth and feeling the first flutters of life, realizing that she was growing a baby inside her" (115). With an affective matching taking place, the narrator is able to empathize with her mother: "Now that I was growing this alien inside me, I could understand better my mother's urges during those first few months, and I wondered whether she had been trying to escape her husband or me, the child-to-be" (120). Moreover, during her own process of labour, Fajardo then imagines her mother's experience with her delivery: "I thought of my mother in labor in what was then a fairly primitive hospital in Popayán [a city in Colombia], two hundred miles from a big city, three thousand miles from her mother" (129). The experience after birth also helps to build bridges in their relationship. Given that she had to take antidepressants, she can understand better how a child may not bring the immediate happiness others talk about: "I imagine her, with a twinge of the same postpartum depression I later experienced" (33). As mentioned earlier in this chapter, when a daughter becomes a mother, there can sometimes occur the forgiveness of her own mother. In Fajardo's case, it is evident, as she admits: "Despite the fact that my mother did the unthinkable—to steal away a child from a father—she owned that choice. And because she apologized, there was nothing for me but forgive her. To forgive her meant to accept my mother with all her flaws, to love her despite them and because of them" (173). Becoming a mother of a daughter enables Fajardo to see her mother's choices as those of someone who sought to protect her loved ones and her own self. Through a process of other-oriented perspective-taking and self-other differentiation, the author of *Magical Realism for Non-Believers* integrates all aspects of her mother's experience that led to raising her daughter as a single mother.

## Discussion

Moraga and Fajardo also empathize with their mothers when they engage in critiques of the multiple oppressions they and their mothers experience. In their writings. we observe what such feminists as Patricia Hill Collins, Alice Walker, bell hooks, Audre Lorde, and Gloria Anzaldúa have highlighted: the multiple aspects of identity that intersect and influence the experience of motherhood, particularly for North American women of African and Hispanic descent. As Collins explains: "Ongoing tensions characterize efforts to mold the institution of Black motherhood to benefit intersecting oppressions of race, gender, class, sexuality, and nation and efforts by African-American women to define and value our own experiences with motherhood" (176). For her part, in the fourth edition of *This Bridge Called My Back,* Moraga reiterates the definition of "theory in the flesh," which "makes sense of the seeming paradoxes of our lives; that complex confluence of identities—race, class, gender, sexuality—systemic to women of color oppression and liberation" (xix). Although the volume is not exclusively about motherhood, several of the authors talk about their experiences with their mothers. For example, Moraga does it in her poem "For the

Color of My Mother" (10-11). Gloria Anzaldúa examines the confluence of identities and highlights the influence of her mother, and mythical mothers, on her identity as a Chicana "border woman" in *Borderlands*. In this way, with their writings and activism, these theorists have redefined what it means to be mothers, as women of colour, in their particular communities.

As I mentioned before, memoir writing is a political act. In regard to rearticulating the meaning of motherhood for Latinx communities, the memoirs examined here give a voice to women as daughters and mothers who denounce oppression. For example, Moraga highlights that she and her mother come from the working class: "My mother and I share this: the hands and arms of worker women—stove burns and the abraded skin of decades of bleach and household detergent; the calluses of yard work, rose thorns, and heavy lifting" (167). She also acknowledges her family's denial of their Indigenous ancestry as a result of internalized colonialism: "What la familia Moraga shares historically with multiple generations of Mexicans and Mexican Americans is the denial of our Native origins" (179). For this reason, Moraga is pleased when her mother brings up in a conversation that she indeed has this ancestry: "It wasn't until the last years of her life that my mother admitted aloud what I already knew from the character of her mexicanismo, that as a mestiza she was also 'indian' … *Bueno, también soy india*" (181). For Moraga, this admission means a reclaiming of the often-erased Indigenous legacy for people of Latin American origins.

Unlike Moraga's mother, Nancy is privileged because of the colour of her skin. She would experience oppression as a foreign woman in Colombia married to a man who disregarded fidelity. She then would become a single mother in the US in a time when it was not popular. Fajardo reflects on this fact to highlight her mother's agency in raising a child by herself: "Mother and daughter, the two of us forg[ed] a path during a time when the phenomenon of single mother was new. In the 1980s, only one in ten children was raised by a single parent, and those (mostly) women were often vilified for their single status, seen as freeloaders or welfare moms" (63). For this reason, for Fajardo, going to Colombia and digging through her family history allowed her to better understand her mother, more so than the father with whom she longed to reconnect.

## Conclusion

These memoirs by Moraga and Fajardo are matrifocal narratives that emphasize the mother-daughter relationship as one full of possibility for mutual understanding when empathy is in place. As these daughters become mothers, an affective matching process allows them to think of their mothers as women with flaws and virtues like themselves. The sudden clarity afforded by going through similar experiences as their mothers does not blur completely their realization that they (Moraga and Fajardo) are separate individuals who now have the responsibility of their own children. Both Moraga and Fajardo become mothers but choose to live in a way different from their own mothers while acknowledging their love, admiration, and respect for them. These accounts, based on lived experience, allow us to envision mothers and daughters as allies in the redefinition of motherhood for Latinx parenting.

## Endnotes

1. I use the expression "matrifocal narrative" as conceived by Andrea O'Reilly, who defines it as "one in which a mother plays a role of cultural and social significance and in which motherhood is thematically elaborated and valued, and is structurally central to the plot" (5-6).

## Works Cited

Anzaldúa, Gloria. *Borderlands/La Frontera: The New Mestiza*. 4th ed. Aunt Lute Books, 2012.

Cantú, Norma E. "Memoir, Autobiography, Testimonio (Part IV: Literary Forms)." *The Routledge Companion to Latino/a Literature*, edited by Suzanne Bost and Frances R. Aparicio, Routledge, 2015, pp. 310-22.

Chodorow, Nancy. *The Reproduction of Mothering: Psychoanalysis and the Sociology of Gender*. University of California Press, 1978.

Collins, Patricia Hill. *Black Feminist Thought: Knowledge, Consciousness, and the Politics of Empowerment*. 2nd ed. Routledge, 2000.

Coplan, Amy. "Understanding Empathy: Its Features and Effects."

*Empathy: Philosophical and Psychological Perspectives*, edited by Amy Coplan and Peter Goldie, Oxford University Press, 2011, pp. 3-18.

Esguerra, Catalina. "Diasporic Home: US Colombian Belonging and Becoming in Patricia Engel's *Vida*." *Latino Studies*, vol. 18, no. 3, 2020, pp. 343-62.

Fajardo, Anika. *Magical Realism for Non-Believers: A Memoir of Finding Family*. University of Minnesota Press, 2019.

Friday, Nancy. *My Mother/My Self: The Daughter's Search for Identity*. 20th ed. Delta, 1997.

Herrera, Cristina. *Contemporary Chicana Literature: (Re) Writing the Maternal Script*. Cambria Press, 2015.

Hunt, Lynn. *Inventing Human Rights: A History*. W. W. Norton and Co., 2007.

Lanzoni, Susan Marie. *Empathy: A History*. Yale University Press, 2018.

Moraga, Cherríe. *Native Country of the Heart: A Memoir*. Farrar, Straus and Giroux, 2019.

Moraga, Cherríe, and Gloria Anzaldúa, editors. *This Bridge Called My Back: Writings by Radical Women of Color*. 4th ed. SUNY Press, 2015.

Morson, Gary Saul. *Prosaics and Other Provocations: Empathy, Open Time, and the Novel*. Academic Studies Press, 2013.

Oatley, Keith. *The Passionate Muse: Exploring Emotion in Stories*. Oxford University Press, 2012.

O'Reilly, Andrea. *Matricentric Feminism: Theory, Activism, and Practice*. Demeter Press, 2016. Print.

Rich, Adrienne. *Of Woman Born: Motherhood as Experience and Institution*. Norton, 1976.

Weigel, Sigrid. "The Heterogeneity of Empathy." *Empathy: Epistemic Problems and Cultural-Historical Perspectives of a Cross-Disciplinary Concept*, edited by Vanessa Lux and Sigrid Weigel, Palgrave Macmillan, 2017, pp. 1-23.

Chapter 14

# Maternal Haunting in Elisa Albert's *After Birth*

Rachel Williamson

*We're supposed to have mothers, I say. We're supposed to have sisters. But what if you don't have a mother?*

—Elisa Albert, *After Birth* (69)

Feminist theory has long had a complex and difficult relationship with motherhood, characterized by contradiction and competing impulses. Interestingly, however, the same cannot be said of daughters. Instead, there is a rich tradition of work that seeks to analyze and unpack the daughter's experience and connection (or lack thereof) with her mother. Although such work is undeniably important, it inevitably tends to fall prey to privileging the child's perspective at the expense of the mother's own subjectivity. Consequently, recent years have seen both the growth in maternal studies as a legitimate academic discipline as well as an explosive proliferation in popular culture and literary texts that seek to explore motherhood. Although these may vary in style, form, and tone, certain narrative beats and tropes echo throughout them, including an exploration of the often fraught mother-daughter relationship. Mothers are, of course, also daughters, but as contemporary scholars are increasingly pointing out, a mother's reactivation of and return to her own childhood experiences is fundamentally different because she is fundamentally different.

Elisa Albert's caustic, vitriolic novel *After Birth* is, in many ways, representative of these contemporary cultural impulses. It employs a first-person narrative told from the point of view of new mother and feminist academic, Ari. Like other literary texts seeking to foreground the maternal perspective, the novel features an episodic, fragmented structure, expressed in short staccato syntax juxtaposed with long meandering sentences. Although the cumulative effect of Ari's careening, freewheeling thoughts can seem at times overly ruminative and digressive, the structure is skilfully deployed to mirror the disjointed and transformed subjective experience Ari undergoes as a result of maternity, which contributes towards her sense of being increasingly disconnected from the world around her. For Ari, motherhood is experienced as a site of trauma, a catastrophic shattering, in which having a baby is "exactly like when someone dies" (174); the death here, of course, being that of the prebaby self. This depiction of maternity as a crisis of identity—an undoing—is an increasingly recognizable trope in maternal texts and accounts for much of Ari's fury and ambivalence. Indeed, she mournfully points out the following: "Maybe you make a living, maybe you get to know yourself on your own terms. Maybe you have adventures, heartbreak. Maybe you nurture ambition. Maybe you explore your sexuality. And then: unceremoniously sliced in fucking half, handed a new-born, home to your little isolation tank, to get on with it" (174).

Here, Ari paints motherhood to be a form of conflict between the pre- and postbaby self or, put another way, between the "competing, yet intertwined needs" of a mother and her child (LaChance Adams 13). As Ari herself notes, this situation then becomes drastically exacerbated by our "little isolation tanks" (124) and the expectation made of today's mothers to "get on with it" (124). This can be taken as symptomatic of both neoliberalism and Sharon Hays's now famous ideology of intensive mothering, which not only valorizes "child-rearing methods that are child-centred, expert-guided, emotionally absorbing, labour-intensive, and financially expensive" (122) but also insists on holding individual mothers accountable. Within this schema of fierce individualism, Ari's maternal ambivalence is, consequently, also experienced as a profound lack of connection with other women. As such, although the events of the novel unfold over Ari's first year of motherhood, the narrative circles back further still to examine her earlier adolescent experiences, female friendships, and, crucially, the toxic relationship with her manic and abusive mother, Janice. This latter relationship is depicted in *After Birth* as a series of imagined conversations between Ari and the ghost of her now-deceased mother. In framing the mother-daughter relationship thus, Albert illuminates the extent to which new mothers are haunted by their own mothers through both a reactivation of their infantile and childhood experiences and a daughter's renewed longing for her own connection to the maternal. Additionally, this haunting also exposes the surveillance that contemporary mothers are routinely subjected to via the cultural valorization of intensive mothering. Tellingly, as Ari develops an intimate friendship with another new mother, Mina, she is haunted less and less by her own mother. This plot point suggests that the biological mother-daughter relationship Ari longs for can, in fact, be superseded by connection with other surrogate maternal figures, thus providing a means to survive maternal ambivalence and carve out a maternal subjectivity. Much like the theoretical and literary feminist perspectives preceding it, *After Birth* can, therefore, be read as a text that recognizes the significance of the mother-daughter relationship. As we shall see, however, it differs radically in its revisionary effort to foreground the maternal rather than the child's point of view.

## Daughtercentric Texts and Perspectives

The prioritizing of the child over the mother is a trend that can be mapped in both feminist theory and women's writing. This is especially true in feminist psychoanalytic accounts of motherhood, which have sought to unravel femininity from maternity in order to better understand the daughter's position. In many ways, this meant rejecting the "phallic logic" of Freud's trajectory of normal, desirable female development to reimagine the development of sexual difference through a return to the maternal body as the site of pre-Oedipal plenitude. Given that traditional Freudian theory is founded upon the matricidal rejection of the mother and subsequent valorization of motherhood as the ultimate end goal in heterosexual female development, this meant that for a long time, "no one had really noticed the mother-daughter relationship" (Chodorow 340). As such, this paucity gave rise to a feminist recasting of traditional Freudian models, particularly the Oedipal plot, in order to more adequately theorize the female trajectory towards attaining subjectivity.

Nancy Chodorow's 1978 seminal text, *The Reproduction of Mothering*, sits neatly within this revisionary work as an attempt to answer why it is that women mother. It recognizes the centrality of mothering to women's lives and also the absence of analysis surrounding it. As such, it emphasizes the previously neglected mother-daughter relationship while accounting for a specifically female identity that is, importantly, not perceived as traumatic and founded upon lack. Although largely celebrated and recognized as canonical, Chodorow's work has also been widely critiqued for a variety of reasons, including, of especial interest here, the psychoanalytic tendency to elide mothers' experiences and subjectivity in general, focusing instead on the child's (or in feminist reworkings the daughter's) perspective. Similarly, poststructural feminists share an effort to correct the Freudian neglect of the mother by reinscribing the maternal function back into the psychoanalytic story of subjecthood. However, unlike Chodorow, they are informed by and work within a Lacanian tradition, emphasizing the role of language in the development of subjectivity and sexual difference. By focusing on language thus, they seek to trouble phallocentrism by imagining a feminine and maternal site that exists a priori to the Law of the Father and the instantiation of Lacan's symbolic order. As critics have noted, however, in doing so they problematically return to the maternal body through the daughter (Kaplan 37), thus leaving the mother herself mute (Rozmarin 245). What emerges from the criticisms of these different feminist engagements with psychoanalysis is the continuation of the long-standing matricidal convention of privileging the child's perspective. As such, the mother's identity as subject is erased, described instead as "function," "object," "metaphor," "vanishing point," "container," and "mirror."

Women's literary contributions have likewise tended to silence maternal subjects. Writing in 1989, Marianne Hirsch turns to the story of Oedipus Rex (as an example of both classical literature but also psychoanalytic theory) to point out that, crucially, we never hear from Jocasta—that is, the maternal point of view. She notes that although feminists might have been busy scrutinizing and revising the Oedipal plot, few writers or theorists were interested in the desires, thoughts, experiences, or development of the mother herself (2). Consequently, not only does maternity have a long tradition of being imagined in conventional, essentialized, and narrow representational terms, but also the mother as subject—complex, contradictory, thinking, desiring, and speaking—remains largely absent or silent (see also Podnieks and O'Reilly 5, 12). This is not to say that mother figures cannot be found in literature; they are not literally absent but rather they are an example of E. Ann Kaplan's "absent presence" (3). Similarly, Brenda O. Daly and Maureen T. Reddy draw on Hirsch's influential thesis to observe that "even in women's accounts of motherhood, maternal perspectives are strangely absent" (1). Instead, as per the psychoanalytic treatment of the maternal, "texts about mothers, mothering, and motherhood, even in those written by feminists who are mothers" (1) have foregrounded the daughter's perspective, producing daughtercentric stories wherein we "learn less about what it is like to mother than about what it is like to be mothered" (2). Daly and Reddy take up Hirsch's challenge that in order to tell the story of Jocasta, Oedipus's mother, from her perspective, we "would have to begin with the mother" (Hirsch 5)—an imperative that Elizabeth Podnieks and Andrea O'Reilly contend is being taken seriously by both maternal scholars and women writers today (2).

Although I agree that contemporary representations are indeed engaged in an endeavour to "unmask motherhood" (Podnieks and O'Reilly 3), it is important to recognize that becoming a mother does not simply stop one from being a daughter; rather "the figure of the mother ... is always both mother and daughter" (Hirsch 12). Her maternal experiences and choices are inevitably overlaid with sublimated past memories of being mothered. As per Ari's experience in *After Birth,* these might resurface as a longing for an absent maternal figure or even as negative psychic reactivations of a hostile mother-daughter relationship. Such representations are therefore important in providing a new, hitherto silenced, perspective on the mother-daughter relationship—specifically that of the maternal subject.

## Returning to One's Mother

Although Chodorow's work might have been flawed in prioritizing the daughter's perspective and subjectivity over the maternal one, her thesis remains relevant in that it is founded upon the notion that women experience themselves as being in relation to their mothers and psychosocial histories. At play here, then, is the new mother's reactivation of her own infantile past as a daughter, an experience that contemporary scholar Alison Stone argues is unique and specific to mother-child relations (134). For Stone, this remembering is prompted by interbodily corporeality and the "distinctive present context of relentless, intimate caring for a pre-verbal infant" (133). She posits that these memories often resurface as fragments, frequently experienced as dreams or intrusions, and manifest in the unconscious or at the level of the body—perhaps even as a sleep-deprived haunting, as is the case in *After Birth*. As Stone notes, for some mothers, this calling up of the past can trigger negative memories wherein mothers may "feel overpowered and overwhelmed by their own mothers," subjected to repudiation and judgment (141). However, she points out that unlike infants, mothers have the ability to "try to comprehend this past and make sense of it, transforming how they speak and narrate so as to integrate the past into the present and to generate significance from that past" (141). Stone's contribution to feminist work on the mother-daughter relationship is, therefore, critical in that it acknowledges the ways in which the maternal subject position and point of view is influenced by—but distinct from—the daughter's position; indeed, she argues instead that "Mothering is a variation on being a daughter, insofar as the mother replays with her child her own maternal past. Yet this maternal replaying of the past is a replaying with a difference" (5).

As we shall see, this process of remembering is central to Ari's own maternal experience, reactivated by the bodily work of caring for her son. Although Ari already experiences motherhood as a crisis of identity, the traumatic haunting presence (and loss) of her own mother exacerbates her feelings of loneliness, anger, and disconnection. Reconciling herself with this past (Stone's act of "integrat[ing] the past into the present" [141]) is therefore a crucial step towards staking out a subject position for herself that is informed by her status as daughter to Janice but also mother to Walker. The representation of this doubled subject position becomes even more prescient when we consider both the psychoanalytic and literary tendency to submerge the maternal subject beneath the body of the daughter.

## Maternal Haunting

Whereas mothers have traditionally haunted the margins of literature as spectral outlines rather than fully realized characters, *After Birth* enacts this haunting quite literally. Early on in the novel, we learn that Janice was sick for the entirety of Ari's childhood and died from cancer when Ari was a teenager. To the prepubescent Ari, her mother's death was not only a "treacherous" act of abandonment (56) but also deeply "embarrassing" (57), eliciting unwanted pity from her peers and family members. Tellingly, Ari's rejection of empathy from, and connection with, others preempts both her loneliness in motherhood and also her inability to sustain a female friendship—a difficulty that stems back to the central loss she experienced as a child. This is complicated further by the fact that Janice was euphemistically understood to be "moody," which is crudely translated by the nine-year-old Ari to mean "a bitch from hell" (48). Indeed, she describes her mother as physically violent, capable of using "force and terror for shits and giggles" (48). Despite this, however, Ari's recollections are complex and fraught, clouded by a yearning for the maternal presence that was missing from most of her life. Significantly, this becomes even more pronounced for Ari on becoming a mother herself.

The reactivation of childhood memories that Ari experiences manifests in a series of psychic encounters outside her cognitive control and, as per Stone's thesis, surfaces in response to the interbodily corporeal work of caring for a newborn. Thus, the first haunting occurs when she is breastfeeding Walker "one night, late, almost morning" (65). As any new mother would testify, this can be a dangerous, lonely time, when sleep deprivation and the disruption to circadian rhythms combine to amplify one's sense of disconnect and isolation from normal daily life. The imagined conversation therefore plays out like a surreal, nightmarish hallucination, informed by Ari's exhaustion but also her complex vacillation between her roles as daughter and mother. As befits Ari's recollections of her mother as cruel and judgmental, Janice appears here to be critical of everything Ari is doing: She questions Ari's decision to breastfeed, criticizes the mess in the house, makes fun of Walker's name, and challenges Ari on her lack of progress on her doctoral dissertation. When Walker picks up on Ari's distress and regurgitates breast milk over her, Janice reacts with scornful condemnation and berates Ari: "*Take a shower! Change your clothes. Jesus. Make yourself something to eat. Any opportunity to fall apart, this one. Have you looked in a mirror lately? What is the big deal, here? Get it together. Honestly"* (67). It is important at this point to remember that Janice is not literally there; rather, she is both a manifestation of Ari's memories and an internalized voice of judgment. Within a psychoanalytic framework, this is, in itself, an interesting revision of the law of the father, attributing more significance to the maternal function than usual.

Furthermore, Janice's spectral figure can also be read as an actualization of contemporary motherhood discourses and ideologies that work to construct a valorized maternal norm. These are underpinned by the essentialist belief that motherhood is biologically desired, natural, instinctive, and ultimately fulfilling to women (Hays 129), thus creating a set of exhausting expectations demanded of mothers. As we can see in Janice's comments, this is predicated not just on a mother's ability to care for her baby but to "get it together" more generally, as per the neoliberal fetishization of the individual (hence, Janice's insistence that Ari should manage herself better, especially in regard to her body and appearance—the signifier par excellence of feminine success). Given that Janice is a product of Ari's imagining, she also reflects the extent to which Ari has problematically accepted these impossible standards, pitting them against herself in a panopticon of self-surveillance. Janice is, in effect, a representation of Ari's own feelings of maternal guilt and failure. Her unconscious reproduction of a culturally condoned maternal norm, against which she deems herself a failure, therefore reflects the oppressive hold such idealized, unobtainable visions of maternity have over women. It is this that renders ordinary maternal ambivalence unmanageable—a situation that is heightened further still for Ari by the fact that it appears to be voiced by her mother, a figure who is meant to represent safety, security, and comfort.

Given the extent to which Ari's internalized cultural condemnations of herself as a mother echo her experience of being mothered, *After Birth*'s instances of maternal haunting can be taken as a "return to this infantile position" (Stone 136). Consequently, they prompt Ari to "feel again as she felt about her own mother in her early childhood ... punished, deprived, or restricted" (126). However, although these memories may resurface subconsciously, adult mothers differ from young children in that they are able to reframe their childhood experiences and relations with their mothers "into narrative and render them meaningful" (147). In Ari's case, this manifests as an effort to suppress her anger, even as she finds herself chafing against the infantile emotional response her mother's chastisement elicits. Furthermore, she strives to actively reject her own mother's repudiation and judgment in her interactions with Walker, noting that she "didn't want to be that way around him, no flash of anger" (66). Juxtaposed against Janice's brittle viciousness, Walker seems especially precious and vulnerable, in need of her protection, but this is also the way in which she can reframe her own experiences of being mothered: "*I wanted this to be a good thing,* I hissed. *A fresh start. A new thing*" (66). Significantly, it would seem that part of the "new thing" Ari is hoping for is a renewed engagement with her own mother as alluded to by her efforts to connect with her mother through her son. Thus, we see her tentatively offer Walker up, a gift that might transcend the toxicity of their own mother-daughter relationship: "*This is my son,* I said, gazing at him to be spared her. *This is Walker. Isn't he beautiful?* The big eyes, so liquid and good. You couldn't help but smile, be filled with the presence of whatever the hell we can all agree on" (66).

The desire to connect with her mother—to find something "we can all agree on"—becomes even more pronounced in the following hallucinatory exchange. At this point, Ari's ambivalence is on the brink of becoming abjectly unmanageable; indeed, she wonders: "How I would make it through the next few days. I feared I might not make it through the next few hours" (96). Consequently, when Janice appears, Ari pleads with her to "please be a little bit maternal for a few minutes" (96), exposing her own need to be a daughter—to be comforted and supported in her role as a new mother, despite the historical deprivations she has felt at the hands of Janice. Perhaps not surprisingly given her academic background, Ari is herself mindful of some of the complexities and contradictions inherent to her simultaneous yearning for and rejection of Janice as a maternal presence. Indeed, she notes: "There was still a small openness in my heart for her, it was true. A pinprick from which blood or love or whatever still flowed. She was part of me, after all. I was part of her. No matter what, it was true. She was in me" (96).

Of particular interest here is Ari's recognition of herself as a subject in relation with and formed by the alterity of others. Her acknowledgment that "she was part of me, after all. I was part of her" not only recognizes the critical role the mother plays in a daughter's life but also challenges traditional Cartesian understandings of the self as discrete, coherent, and stable. Instead, here, the maternal subject is depicted as a position that resists singularity, emphasizing plurality and movement instead. Given that much of *After Birth* consists of Ari recounting her difficulties sustaining meaningful connection and friendship with other women, the empathetic "openness in my heart" (96) (even if it is a small one) signals a radical shift in perspective for her. Although this change is specifically related to her own mother-daughter relationship, it is important to note that it is on becoming a mother herself that it occurs: Ari is a daughter "with a difference" (Stone 5), hence the return here to her mother and the replaying of childhood memories is also fundamentally different. Thus, not only is motherhood for Ari a site of trauma, crisis, and ambivalence (as reflected through the episodes of maternal haunting, which are themselves symptomatic of contemporary mothering ideologies), but it is also a space imbued with the ethical potential to facilitate connection with others. This is especially apparent in Ari's friendship with a new mother, Mina—a relationship that ultimately comes to supplant Ari's longing for a mother-daughter connection of her own.

## Surrogate Mothers

In her article "Mother-Writing and the Narrative of Maternal Subjectivity," Suzanne Juhasz posits that it is often difficult to unravel whether a text is better classified as a "mother-text" or a "daughter-text" (398), since "not only is the daughter who becomes a mother still the daughter of her mother, but her daughterhood is part of her motherhood" (399). Despite this, she argues that although many contemporary literary texts about motherhood persist in unpacking the daughter's experience, they should not be mistaken for "daughter-writing" (400); rather, they can be read as maternal in their efforts to foreground maternal subjectivity as "multiple rather than split" (420; see also Hirsch 247). These texts recognize the maternal subject position as having the potential to reconcile a woman's many selves and thus account for her relationships with both her own children and her mother. However, in order for this to be enacted successfully, it requires recognition from another maternal figure. Although this is typically received by a new mother from her own biological mother, Juhasz looks at literary precedents that suggest it can also be performed by a surrogate maternal figure. This recognition then becomes a means for surviving maternal ambivalence, if we take ambivalence to be a crisis of identity and the splitting of the pre- and postbaby self. Given Ari's experience of motherhood as a metaphoric death, combined with her inability to hold down female friendships, she is, as we have seen, especially vulnerable to the common yearning for one's own mother ("*We're supposed to have mothers,* I say" [69]), hence the recurring appearance of her mother's ghost in her more desperate moments. As per Juhasz's argument, however, *After Birth* makes the case that the recognition Ari is craving can, in fact, be derived from connection with alternative maternal stand-ins—in this instance Mina Morris, a heavily pregnant poet and 1980s girl-band bassist.

Although the friendship begins much like many of Ari's earlier failed ones (with her developing a crush on Mina and obsessively idolizing her), it quickly develops into a more profound connection, based on mutuality and shared interbodily corporeality. In part, this can be attributed to the nearness in ages of their babies and common maternal experiences of birth, sleep deprivation, and breastfeeding. More specifically, however, it is a result of the taboo-breaking shared nursing that becomes so central to the women's relationship. On visiting Mina in the weeks following her son's birth, Ari discovers that Zev is "failing, in the parlance of infants, to thrive" (78). Likewise, Mina herself is exhausted and in pain—"swaying, bouncing on the soles of her feet, babbling like a brook for anything else … speaking in tongues" (78). Mina is struggling to latch Zev successfully, and feeding is proving problematic, resulting in impending mastitis and a furiously hungry baby. Keenly mindful of her own desperate need for help during the early stages of motherhood, Ari begins by making food for Mina before proceeding to nurse Zev herself. What begins as a temporary answer quickly evolves into a pattern of comfort and reciprocity. The two women soon begin spending all their days together, listening to music, and nursing one another's babies. (As an older baby, Walker is able to latch more independently, thus helping Mina to establish feeding.) Although this solution is an unusual one in contemporary white, Western society, potentially provoking discomfort, even disgust,

Ari is quick to point out that "this is what women have done since time immemorial. We've rediscovered normal. No sitting home alone going quietly insane, thankyouverymuch. This is my motherfucking dissertation" (105). Not only does the relationship therefore provide an antidote to Ari's ambivalence, but, tellingly, as the friendship develops, Ari is also haunted less and less by her own mother, thus suggesting that the desire to return to one's own mother is, in fact, more a need for connection and recognition in this drastically altered subject position. Ari underscores this point by describing her identification with Mina as "like a big old bell I can feel ringing in the best part of me." She continues: "I had no idea there was so much room in me, what a pleasant place I turn out to be. Recognition. Reunion. A light on that's been out a long time" (111).

In following Juhasz, we can see here that Mina has functioned as a surrogate maternal figure, filling the gap left by the death of Ari's own mother. In witnessing Ari's corporeal maternal work, she has provided the recognition Ari craved as a daughter. Furthermore, however, she has also been daughter to Ari, who has taken on the role of carer for Mina. Their relationship can therefore be characterized by movement and liminality, highlighting the radical nature of maternal subjectivity as multiple and in conversation with the alterity of the other: "One entity, her and me. One body. Boundaries are nothing but a refusal of life and love" (138). Whereas this dissolution of boundaries is often applied to the mother in her dyadic relation to her infant, Albert severs it from its essentialist implications to instead suggest that the maternal can function as a space of ethical potential and provide a framework of alternative ways of being in relation with others.

## Conclusion

Without doubt, *After Birth* is clearly invested in mapping the significance of the mother-daughter relationship. The long-term psychic ramifications of Ari's toxic relationship with her hostile, abusive mother informs much of the ruminative, retrospective narrative, evidently foreclosing Ari's ability to connect meaningfully with other women. Additionally, the episodes of maternal haunting suggest that Ari's infantile and childhood memories of being mothered might have negatively affected her ability to mother herself. Accordingly, *After*

*Birth* could, at first glance, be considered an example of a daughtercentric text. As contemporary maternal scholars like Alison Stone and Suzanne Juhasz point out, however, mothers are also daughters, and, as such, their daughterhood informs their experiences of motherhood. In that regard, *After Birth* can be better understood as part of a growing literary trend to unpack the mother-daughter relationship from the perspective of the mother herself, thus refusing the traditional tendency to prioritize the child's point of view. Albert's novel is therefore invested in chronicling Ari's efforts to "integrate the past into the present and to generate significance from that past" (Stone 141). Through accepting the formative impact of the mother-daughter relationship, while rejecting her mother's repudiation, Ari can seek the recognition she yearns from an alternative maternal stand-in (Mina). In doing so, she not only resists succumbing to an unmanageable maternal ambivalence, exacerbated by loneliness and isolation, but also forges a maternal subjectivity founded upon multiplicity: She is both mother *and* daughter, leading her to tentatively conclude that "maybe I'm better" (194).

## Works Cited

Albert, Elisa. *After Birth*. Vintage, 2016.

Chodorow, Nancy J. "Reflections on *The Reproduction of Mothering* — Twenty Years Later." *Studies in Gender and Sexuality*, vol. 1, no 4, 2000, pp. 337-48.

Daly, Brenda O., and Maureen T. Reddy. *Narrating Mothers: Theorizing Maternal Subjectivities*. University of Tennessee Press, 1991.

Hays, Sharon. *The Cultural Contradictions of Motherhood*. Yale University Press, 1998.

Hirsch, Marianne. *The Mother/Daughter Plot: Narrative, Psychoanalysis, Feminism*. Indiana University Press, 1989.

Juhasz, Suzanne. "Mother-Writing and the Narrative of Maternal Subjectivity." *Studies in Gender and Sexuality*, vol. 4, no. 4, 2003, pp. 395-425.

Kaplan, E. Ann. *Motherhood and Representation: The Mother in Popular Culture and Melodrama*. Routledge, 1992.

LaChance Adams, Sarah. *Mad Mothers, Bad Mothers, and What a "Good"*

*Mother Would Do: The Ethics of Ambivalence*. Columbia University Press, 2016.

Podnieks, Elizabeth, and Andrea O'Reilly. *Textual Mothers/Maternal Texts: Motherhood in Contemporary Women's Literatures*. Wilfrid Laurier University Press, 2010.

Rozmarin, Miri. "Staying Alive: Matricide and the Ethical-Political Aspect of Mother-Daughter Relations." *Studies in Gender and Sexuality*, vol. 17, no. 4, 2016, pp. 242-53.

Stone, Alison. *Feminism, Psychoanalysis, and Maternal Subjectivity*. Routledge, 2012.

# Notes on Contributors

**Renée E. Mazinegiizhigoo-kwe Bédard** is of Anishinaabeg (Ojibwe/Nipissing/Omàmiwinini) and French Canadian ancestry. She is a member of Okikendawdt (Dokis First Nation). She holds a PhD from Trent University in Indigenous studies. Currently, she is an assistant professor at Western University in the Faculty of Education. Her areas of publication include practices of Anishinaabeg motherhood, maternal philosophy, and spirituality, along with environmental issues, women's rights, Indigenous Elders, Anishinaabeg artistic expressions, and Indigenous education.

**Mali Collins** is a doula, childbirth educator, and an assistant professor of African American studies at American University, writing at the intersections of memory, public health, and black reproductive life.

**Inês Faro** is a PhD student in comparative literature at the Université de Montréal and holds a doctoral grant from the FQRSC. She is also an advanced candidate at the Canadian Institute of Psychoanalysis—QE. She is interested in women's self-representations in the intersection of literary studies and psychoanalysis.

**Joan Garvan's** doctoral thesis *Maternal Ambivalence in Contemporary Australia: Navigating Equity and Care* is available to view at www.maternalhealthandwellbeing.com She has offered online professional development courses, webinars, and continues to work as an advocate for improved early years health and welfare services with Maternal Health Matters. Joan was a founding member of Maternal Scholars Australia (formerly AMIRCI) and has presented at conferences in Australia, New York, Toronto, and Florence.

**Sylvia Griffin** is a Sydney-based multidisciplinary artist and writer whose work addresses trauma, memory, and history. She holds a PhD from Sydney University and has contributed to several peer-reviewed journals, books, and conferences. She has exhibited nationally and internationally, received various prizes, grants and scholarships, and has been shortlisted for several national awards. Her work is held in collections both nationally and internationally.

**Lauren Hansen** is a senior lecturer at Deakin University in Melbourne, Australia. She is particularly interested in the intersection of the self, education, and employment. Lauren's practice experience includes working with mothers in the community and private practice to reengage with education and meaningful employment.

**Jameka Hartley**, PhD, is an interdisciplinary Black feminist scholar and poet. Her work centres on issues of Black motherhood, popular cultural representations of Black women, child to adult outcomes, and stigma. Her simultaneous identities of being a daughter and a mother shape both her life and her scholarship.

**Allegra Holmes**, a matricentric feminist artist, makes and writes about artwork that destabilizes patriarchal notions of domesticity and mothering, upholding these things as not just worthy artistic subject matter but also as significant modes of feminist praxis.

**Kandee Kosior** is a children's programming and outreach librarian. She has a MA in library and information sciences from San Jose State University. Kandee's research interests include feminist mothering, mothers and daughters, and mothers and sons. She is the coeditor of the Demeter Press publication titled *Feminist Parenting*. She treasures the thirty years she has spent with her husband raising their three children.

**Sabela Losada Cortizas** is a Spanish political scientist, writer, and teacher and holds a MA in gender violence. She has researched the effects of structural sexist violence on motherhood, and her latest book deals with the impacts of COVID-19 on working mothers and their families.

# NOTES ON CONTRIBUTORS

**Astrid Lorena Ochoa Campo** is an assistant professor of Spanish at the University of Wisconsin La Crosse. She earned her PhD in Spanish in 2020 from the University of Virginia. Her research interests include contemporary Latin American and Latinx literature; women, gender, and sexuality studies; and motherhood studies.

**Marcia Allen Owens** is professor of environmental science at Florida A&M University. As principal investigator for the National Science Foundation ADVANCE Institutional Transformation grant (HRD-1824287), her research focus is equity for Black women in STEM. She is a graduate of Jackson State University and Emory University (JD, PhD, and MDiv).

**Andi Spark** creates graphic narratives for both print and moving image form, with a focus on stories centred around the female experience. Over more than three decades in the animation field, working internationally across both industry and academia, she has nurtured studios and departments, films, television series, live performances, exhibitions, installations, books, children, and grandchildren. Screen production credits include *Bluey, Li'l Elvis Jones & the Truckstoppers,* and *The Way of the Birds.*

**Cassie Premo Steele**, PhD, is a poet, novelist, and TEDx speaker, who works as a writing coach teaching mindfulness and feminism to women around the world. Her most recent poetry book is *Tongues in Trees: Poems 1994-2017,* and her most recent novel is *The ReSisters.* She is the mother of a grown daughter and grown stepdaughter and recently became a grandmother. She lives with her wife in South Carolina. Her website is www.cassiepremosteele.com

**Rachel Williamson** is an academic and educator based in Christchurch, New Zealand. Her doctoral research investigated representations of maternal ambivalence in contemporary literary and visual texts. Rachel's current research continues to explore the intersections between representational forms and embodied gendered experiences, especially as they pertain to motherhood. Rachel has taught at both secondary and tertiary level and is a senior trainer for a domestic violence specialist agency.

Deepest appreciation to
Demeter's monthly Donors

### Daughters
Rebecca Bromwich
Summer Cunningham
Tatjana Takseva
Debbie Byrd
Fiona Green
Tanya Cassidy
Vicki Noble
Naomi McPherson
Myrel Chernick

### Sisters
Amber Kinser
Nicole Willey
Christine Peets